IT HAPPENED AT GRAND CANYON

It Happened In Series

IT HAPPENED AT
GRAND CANYON

Todd R. Berger

TWODOT®

GUILFORD, CONNECTICUT
HELENA, MONTANA
AN IMPRINT OF THE GLOBE PEQUOT PRESS

To buy books in quantity for corporate use
or incentives, call **(800) 962–0973**
or e-mail **premiums@GlobePequot.com.**

A · TWODOT® · BOOK

Front cover photo: Promotional photo of Ellsworth Kolb holding a graflex camera while suspended in midair by a rope held by Emery Kolb, ca. 1913. Northern Arizona University, Cline Library, Special Collections and Archives, Kolb Collection, NAU.PH.568.840
Back cover photo: The Metz car posing on the canyon rim by the El Tovar Hotel, 1914. Grand Canyon National Park Museum Collection, 16412B
Text design by Nancy Freeborn
Map by M. A. Dubé © Morris Book Publishing, LLC

Library of Congress Cataloging-in-Publication Data
Berger, Todd R., 1968-
  It happened at Grand Canyon/Todd R. Berger.—1st ed.
    p. cm.—(It happened in series)
  Includes bibliographical references and index.
  ISBN-13: 978-0-7627-3839-7
  ISBN-10: 0-7627-3839-1
  1. Grand Canyon (Ariz.)—History—Anecdotes. 2. Grand Canyon National Park (Ariz.)—History—Anecdotes. I. Title.
  F788.B48 2007
  979.1'32—dc22

2006021191

Manufactured in the United States of America
First Edition/Tenth Printing

For Bonnie

CONTENTS

CONTENTS

ACKNOWLEDGMENTS

As a small way of saying thank you, I would like to acknowledge several people who helped get this book to the point where it could be published.

Stephanie Hester of the Globe Pequot Press first suggested the idea of this book to me, and her kind comments and patience as I worked on the manuscript were quite remarkable and are gratefully acknowledged. As an editor myself, I learned a lot from her about working with authors effectively. I also wish to thank Megan Hiller for helping shepherd the book through the publishing process.

Michael F. Anderson, officially a Cultural Resource Specialist at Grand Canyon National Park and unofficially the national park's historian, devoted considerable time to reviewing chapters and commenting on matters of fact. Mike's knowledge of the minutiae of Grand Canyon history is unsurpassed, and I thank him, yet again, for his help.

Grand Canyon Railway historian Al Richmond, former California condor biologist Sophie Osborn, writer Scott Thybony, and Grand Canyon Airlines Chief Pilot Mike McCombs reviewed chapters specific to their expertise and offered critical comments that have improved and tightened the factual information in this book. I am thankful for their willingness to devote time and energy on my behalf.

The Grand Canyon Association's Deputy Director, Pam Frazier, made it possible for me to move to the Grand Canyon four years ago, changing my life in ways that I never imagined. This book would not exist, at least not as authored by me, without her confidence in my abilities and her constant belief that the impossible could be accomplished, piece by piece.

Former Grand Canyon National Park Librarian Susan Eubank helped me find all kinds of obscure material while I was researching the book. The library is now in new, just-as-capable hands, but Susan's 2005 departure for a job in the big city marks a sad moment during my time at Grand Canyon; I thank her nonetheless.

The prior research of several authors and scholars provided critical reference material during the writing of this book. All of the sources of information are noted in the Bibliography, but I would like to call special attention to the work of several individuals, including Eilean Adams, Michael A. Amundson, Michael F. Anderson, Christine Barnes, Arnold Berke, C. Gregory Compton, Brad Dimock, Richard Flint and Shirley Cushing Flint, Michael P. Ghighlieri, Virginia L. Grattan, Stephen Hirst, J. Donald Hughes, Jeff Ingram, Henry Karpinski, Thomas M. Myers, Sophie A. H. Osborn, Byron E. Pearson, Louis Purvis, Al Richmond, Dwight L. Smith, Douglas H. Strong, William C. Suran, Debra Sutphen, Scott Thybony, T. J. Wolf, and Christian C. Young, among others. Many have masterful books out there for which they receive little monetary reward; if a book you see in the Bibliography strikes your fancy, buy a copy, thereby helping support present and future historians of Grand Canyon.

I thank fellow current and former members of the board of the Grand Canyon Historical Society, who have donated huge amounts of time to the cause of furthering knowledge of Grand Canyon history. In particular, I thank Lee Albertson, Mike and Linda Anderson, John Azar, George and Susan Billingsley, Dan and Diane Cassidy, Mike Coltrin, Keith and Nancy Green, Bev Loomis, Jim Ohlman, Al Richmond, Sally Underwood, and Steve Verkamp.

And lastly I thank my wife Bonnie, who put up with a lot of grumpiness as I researched and wrote, and who pulled me back into focus on the job at hand during several episodes of "I'm-a-terrible-writer" thinking. I thank her also for cleaning the litter boxes when I was "busy" writing. Most of all, I thank her for being my best friend and for believing in me when, in my mind, few others did.

GRAND CANYON

NAVAJO INDIAN RESERVATION

Colorado River

Little Colorado River

KAIBAB NATIONAL FOREST

MARBLE CANYON

HOUSE ROCK VALLEY

COCKS COMB

KAIBAB PLATEAU

KAIBAB NATIONAL FOREST

WALHALLA PLATEAU

Cape Royal

Point Imperial

North Rim
Grand Canyon Lodge

Bright Angel Point

GRANITE GORGE

GRAND CANYON VILLAGE

Visitor Center
Park Headquarters

TUSAYAN

Grand Canyon Airport

To FLAGSTAFF
WILLIAMS and

Kaibab Lodge (USFS)
De Motte
North Rim Entrance Station

MUAV CANYON

UPPER GRANITE GORGE

Tapeats Creek

HAVASUPAI INDIAN RESERVATION

COCONINO PLATEAU

Cataract Creek

KANAB CANYON

Havasu Creek

Kanab Creek

Colorado River

Supai
Havasupai Point

Hundred and Fifty Mile Canyon

WHITMORE CANYON

TUCKUP CANYON

KANAB PLATEAU

HUALAPAI INDIAN RESERVATION

PROSPECT VALLEY

NATIONAL CANYON

MOHAWK CANYON

TUCKUP POINT

Colorado River

TOROWEAP VALLEY

Vulcans Throne

LAKE MEAD NATIONAL RECREATION AREA

Whitmore Wash

GRANITE PARK CANYON

N

10 KILOMETERS
10 MILES
0   5

INTRODUCTION

History lies just below the rocky earth throughout the Grand Canyon region. Nearly everywhere visitors to the canyon travel—Grand Canyon Village, Desert View, the North Rim, the inner canyon, the Havasupai Indian Reservation, the Hualapai reservation—those who came before have affected what we see today. The Grand Canyon is a scenic wonder unique to the world, but the highway you drove on or the train you rode to get to the rim, the trail you hiked, the hotel room or campground you slept in, and even the rock wall along the Rim Trail that kept you from stepping over the edge, all have a colorful history.

Naturally, this could be said of just about any place, but at the Grand Canyon, history seems tangible. Kolb Studio, the Bright Angel Trail, the Grand Canyon Railway, El Tovar, Phantom Ranch, the North Rim Lodge, and Hermits Rest are windows to the past, human-built structures that now seem as natural a part of the landscape as the rock layers and the ponderosa pines.

Underlying the broad swath of history on display at the canyon are specific events that shaped what we see today. *It Happened at Grand Canyon* includes some of these events; it is an admittedly subjective collection of stories about the canyon's historic past.

Given the focus on specific events, some historic happenings at the Grand Canyon could not be addressed or are mentioned only in passing. This is not to say larger subjects are not important. On the contrary, the Grand Canyon Enlargement Act of 1975 (which returned almost 200,000 acres of federal land to the Havasupai Tribe), the founding of Grand Canyon National Park, the ancestral Puebloan people, the formation of the rock layers, the antics of early tourism peddlers such as John Hance and W. W. Bass, Harvey Girls at the Fred Harvey establishments, the natural history of Kaibab squirrels versus Abert squirrels, the Hopis' traditional use of the Hopi salt mines within the national park, and the development of commercial river running on the Colorado are all important in the history of the Grand Canyon. But as an "event," they would be difficult to describe in enough detail to give them justice, and therefore separate chapters for these larger subjects are not included in this collection. Readers interested in learning more about some of these topics can find starting points in the bibliography.

The following pages attempt to relay the history of the Grand Canyon through particularly prominent, weird, mysterious, or poignant events. And, of course, the stories are meant to entertain. From the vanished explorers of the 1869 Powell Expedition to the 2003 California condor fledgling, from the 1909 story of an Egyptian tomb in the canyon to the 1992 Grand Canyon crime spree of Danny Ray Horning, the stories are like the structures and trails at the canyon: tangible pieces of history hinting at a larger story.

Whether you are reading this sitting on a bench along the Rim Trail, in the car on your way home from the canyon, in your tent after sundown, or in the easy chair in your living room, the stories in this book reveal Grand Canyon's past. The canyon is a place with a rich and unique history worthy of 10,000 books of this nature. Enjoy.

THE COLORADO RIVER IS
SIX FEET WIDE

- 1540 -

SIXTY-SEVEN YEARS BEFORE THE ENGLISH SETTLED JAMESTOWN, a well-equipped Spanish army led by Francisco Vásquez de Coronado surged northward from Mexico City in search of the Seven Cities of Cíbola and the riches the fabled cities held. Coronado was motivated by tales of vast wealth from Álvar Núñez Cabeza de Vaca, who had walked overland to Mexico City from Florida and described large cities filled with gems and precious metals, and Fray Marcos de Niza, who trekked north to investigate after Cabeza de Vaca voiced his extraordinary claims. Fray Marcos returned from what would later be called New Mexico and testified to the existence of "a great store of gold . . . and a hill of silver" in the Seven Cities of Cíbola.

On February 22, 1540, intoxicated by these tales of bountiful wealth, Coronado headed north with a contingent of more than 300 European soldiers, as well as hundreds of American Indian allies of the Spanish. Coronado undoubtedly looked magnificent in his gilded suit of armor and helmet with a crested plume, astride a horse in full battle armor (if that horse fell in battle, Coronado could quickly switch to one of the twenty-two back-up steeds he had brought along). The well-disciplined fighting force clippity-clopped northward for a full four months until finally reaching the first city of Cíbola, as identified by Fray Marcos, who had unwisely decided to tag along. The city was a Zuni pueblo near the modern New Mexico–Arizona border, but instead of riches, the Coronado expedition found only a village of decidedly more practical stone and mud houses. Despite facing an overwhelming force of mounted, better-equipped, nattily plumed soldiers, the Zunis didn't panic, nor did they become the catalyst for an early Spanish massacre. Instead, they lied.

The Zunis spun tales to the greedy Spaniards of seven far richer cities to the west at Tusayan, better known today as the Hopi pueblos and not to be confused with the commercialized village of the same name just south of the Grand Canyon today. After sending the discredited Fray Marcos packing on the long march back to Mexico City (history has not recorded Fray Marcos's reasons for spinning yarns of vast treasure), Coronado ordered Pedro de Tovar and a contingent of cavalry soldiers to check out the Zuni story. A month later, after attacking and defeating the Hopis, Tovar returned with news that the Hopi pueblos weren't much richer than Cíbola, but that the Hopis had told him of a great river farther to the west. A navigable river through this arid land that potentially could lead to the Sea of Cortez was of great interest to Coronado, and he subsequently ordered García López de Cárdenas and a small group of soldiers to head west and find the river.

Once Cárdenas and his men reached Tusayan, the recently defeated Hopis were understandably eager to get the Spaniards out of the area. Volunteering their services as guides, the Hopis agreed to lead the men to the river. Following a roundabout route, the contingent reached the South Rim of the Grand Canyon in late September 1540, after a twenty-day trek over a relatively short distance as the crow flies. Thus, Cárdenas and his men became the first Europeans to lay their eyes on the Grand Canyon of the Colorado River.

Later historians estimated that the Spaniards reached the canyon's rim somewhere around Lipan Point near Desert View and the eastern edge of the future national park. The Colorado River squiggled in plain sight a mile below their high-elevation viewpoint. The Spaniards correctly estimated that the opposite rim was 8 to 10 miles away, but they not so accurately concluded that the Colorado River couldn't be more than 6 feet across. The river is closer to 300 feet across, and the Hopi guides, perhaps eager to keep the soldiers away from Tusayan, assured the men that the river was much wider than 6 feet. Cárdenas ordered three infantry men to scamper and shimmy their way down to the river after the Hopis pleaded ignorance as to the route to the Colorado and encouraged the naïve soldiers to give it a go on their own (an early version of the Tanner Trail, which led to the river, lay a short distance to the west). The men began their descent of the canyon wall and made impressive progress, working their way down more than 1,500 feet of scree slopes and sheer cliff faces. From their vantage point a third of the way into the canyon, they could clearly see that the Colorado River was indeed a much wider waterway than they had estimated at the rim, but they also determined there was no way to navigate ships along the rapid-punctuated river.

The soldiers returned to the rim, and Cárdenas and his men considered traveling farther west in search of a route to the river. But the Hopis convinced them that rugged country with no water waited to the west, although the Indians were well aware that the Moqui Trail, which linked the Hopis with the Havasupais and Mohaves to the west, was easily negotiable through a temperate forestland. Had they shown the Spaniards this route, the Hopis would have guided them to the lower Colorado River below the Grand Canyon, showing them an overland route to a portion of the river that is navigable all the way to the Sea of Cortez. Instead the Hopis led the soldiers back east after Cárdenas decided further explorations to the west would be fruitless, and the soldiers returned to the Zuni pueblos and the Coronado expedition.

Cárdenas reported to Coronado that a great river did indeed lie to the west, but that it wound through an impenetrable wasteland and was not navigable anyway, concluding that it was therefore of no value to the Spanish. Coronado took in the information, dismissed further western exploration, uprooted his encamped men, and moved them out to the east to overwinter in Texas. In 1542 the army, a little ragged around the edges and very dusty, returned to Mexico City. Coronado had to explain his failure to find the fabled treasure trove in the Seven Cities of Cíbola to Viceroy Antonio de Mendoza, the ruler of Mexico. It was a meeting that didn't go well from Coronado's point of view.

Meanwhile, the Hopis returned to pueblo life. Their extensive "guiding" assistance to the Spaniards brought them some 235 additional years of relatively hassle-free living.

ENTRADA

- 1776 -

THE YEAR 1776 IS WELL KNOWN TO ALL AMERICANS, apart from the young and the inattentive. However, in addition to the outbreak of the Revolutionary War in Concord, Massachusetts, interesting things were happening on the other side of the continent. Pimeria Alta (Arizona) was ruled by Spain (the United States wouldn't gain control of the region until 1848), but many of the deserts, plateaus, and canyons had never been explored by Spaniards—or anybody else of European ancestry. As was the case in so many parts of the world in those days, men (almost exclusively) of religion were tasked with penetrating the wilderness. They could not only bring back information about remote lands, but could convert the "savage" Indians they came across to Christianity. Enter Padre Francisco Tomás Garcés.

In 1767 the viceroy of Mexico ordered fourteen priests to head north for missionary work. Padre Garcés was one of those men, and he arrived at Mission San Xavier del Bac near modern-day Tucson later that year. In pursuit of converts to Christianity, Padre Garcés would make five *entradas* (a formal use of the word meaning "entries into unexplored lands") across the Southwest.

His first four *entradas* kept him well away from the Grand Canyon, but his fifth, begun during the spring of 1776, brought him to Havasu Canyon and then the South Rim. The expedition was led by Don Juan Bautista de Anza and was bound for California (Anza and his men would go on to found San Francisco during this trip). But Padre Garcés stayed behind at what would become Yuma, on the Colorado River in southwestern Arizona.

Padre Garcés was an independent sort. From Yuma, he ventured north alone, eventually reaching the land of the Mohave Indians near modern-day Needles, California. From there, he traveled to Hualapai country, south of the Grand Canyon. His kind hadn't been seen in this country before, but the Hualapai, who the Spanish padre referred to as the *Jaguallapais,* were most hospitable. After Padre Garcés insisted on being led to the Hopi mesas, the Hualapais, who feared the Hopis would kill the Spanish priest, offered to guide the odd, cross-bedecked man into the canyon to meet a tribe hidden within its walls along a stream of blue-green water: the Havasupais.

The route the Hualapai guides followed is roughly the Havasu Trail (also known as the Hualapai Trail) today. Then, as now, it was the easiest way to reach the Havasupai settlement deep within the Grand Canyon. Padre Garcés, suspicious at first, soon heartily partook in Havasupai hospitality.

> *I arrived at the place of our stopping for the night, and as I saw the Jabesua [Havasupai] Indians well supplied with some pieces of red cloth, I suspected therefrom that they might be some of the Apaches who harass these provinces. . . . In spite of this I had no fear, seeing all well content at my arrival. . . .*

*So pleasing was the insistency with which they urged
me to remain in this rancheria [settlement based on
agriculture] that as I found myself constrained perforce
in this place, I had to remain five days; during which
they waited upon me and regaled me with flesh of deer
and cow, with maize, beans, quelites [greens], and
mescal, with all of which they were well provided.*

Despite the feast, Padre Garcés was there on business, and he dutifully preached the gospel to the gathered Havasupais. The Havasupais tolerated the padre's ramblings. However, he didn't make any headway toward conversion for the people of the blue-green water. As his original goal was to reach the Hopi mesas, he decided to move on to the east, saving conversion of the Havasupais for another day.

Padre Garcés asked for a guide to the Hopi mesas, and the Havasupais obliged, leading him out on the Topocoba Trail. Padre Garcés recorded the ascent in his diary:

*I set forth accompanied by five Indians and traveled
south and east, now on horseback, now on foot, but in
both these ways with great exertion, and halted on the
slope of the sierra [mountain] at a scanty aguage
[spring]. In the afternoon I finished the most difficult
part of it. They cause horror, those precipices—and
thereafter traveling north over good ground with much
grass, and many junipers and pines and other trees
among which I went about three leagues, I arrived at a
rancheria which appertains to the Jabesua, whither
had come some of this nation to gather the first of the*

*juniper. The principal Indian offered himself to accom-
pany me next day.*

The area where Padre Garcés and his guides spent the night was
probably Pasture Wash, west of modern-day Grand Canyon Village.
With one remaining Havasupai guide, Padre Garcés headed farther
east the next morning. In his diary, he recorded what he saw:

*June 26. I traveled four leagues southeast, and south,
turning to the east; and halted at the sight of the most
profound caxones [canyon] which ever onward continue; and within these flows the Rio Colorado. There
is seen a very great* sierra, *which in the distance [looks]
blue; and there runs from southeast to northwest a pass
open to the very base, as if the* sierra *were cut artifi-
cially to give entrance to the Rio Colorado into these
lands. I named this singular [pass] Puerto de Bucaréli,
and though to all appearances would not seem to be
very great the difficulty of reaching thereunto, I considered this to be impossible in consequence of the difficult
caxones which intervened.*

For the first time since 1540, a person of European ancestry was
looking at the Grand Canyon. He stood on the South Rim to the west
of modern-day Hermits Rest. The blue sierra he saw in the distance
was likely Navajo Mountain, although some historians have surmised
he was referring to the North Rim itself, which can look like a broad
mountain from the South Rim. Padre Garcés was the first to refer to
the great river in the Grand Canyon as the Rio Colorado, *colorado* the

Spanish word for "colored," a reference to the red sediment that flowed with the current before the construction of Glen Canyon Dam in the 1960s (today, the sediment is held back by the dam). However, Padre Garcés's name for the Grand Canyon, Puerto de Bucaréli, named after the viceroy of Mexico, did not stick.

Padre Garcés could hardly believe his eyes. "I am astonished at the roughness of this country," he wrote, "and at the barrier which nature has fixed therein." That barrier kept them moving east along the rim, and they eventually made it to Oraibi on the Hopi mesas on July 2.

The Hopis were suspicious of the Spaniard, and he was not allowed to enter Hopi houses. He camped outside, but on July 4, the Hopi elders approached and asked him to leave. Padre Garcés recognized that he was unlikely to get the Hopis to listen to his Christian teachings, and he moved on. He returned to Yuma, arriving there on August 27, and then traveled over southern Arizona to San Xavier del Bac.

Sadly, Padre Garcés's life did not end peacefully. Five years after his visit to the Grand Canyon, Quechan (Yuma) Indians rebelled against the Spanish settlers, killing Padre Garcés and several other missionaries.

CHRISTMAS AT THE GRAND CANYON

- 1858 -

Lieutenant Joseph Christmas Ives may have led the first party of white men to reach the bottom of the Grand Canyon, but at first, that wasn't the plan at all. He had in mind finding the head of navigation (the farthest point upriver boats could travel) on the Colorado River. His crew left Fort Yuma, Arizona Territory, on December 30, 1857, aboard the *Explorer,* a steamer built in the East, tested on the Delaware River, judged suitable for the Delaware, and shipped to the mouth of the Colorado River in pieces for Lieutenant Ives's trip. Needless to say, the Colorado is a very different river from the Delaware, and 2 miles upstream from Fort Yuma, the *Explorer* beached on a sandbar.

Lieutenant Ives's crew included the geologist John S. Newberry, topographer and artist Frederick W. von Egloffstein, and the artist Heinrich B. Mollhausen—an impressive collection of talent who would find great use for their skills on this expedition. They also learned new ones, as all hands went to work unloading the beached

Explorer and pushing the now-empty steamship off the sandbar. To Lieutenant Ives's dismay, this elaborate effort was executed within sight of Fort Yuma, and "this sudden check on our progress was affording an evening of great entertainment to those in and out of the garrison." Mentally, he tried to even the score, noting in his official 1861 *Report Upon the Colorado River of the West,* "Fort Yuma is not a place to inspire one with regret at leaving." De-beached, they surged north.

The threat of war with the Mormons of Utah Territory was one reason to seek the head of navigation on the Colorado River. Tensions between the Mormons and the federal government were very high at the time, and many in the government saw war as inevitable. If the head of navigation were far enough north, it could open up a southern supply route for invading federal troops.

Lieutenant Ives and the *Explorer* steamed on, through the territory of the not-so-friendly Yuma Indians and into friendlier Mohave Indian country. Here they ran low on food, and they resorted to eating more corn and beans, and drinking more Colorado River water than they would have preferred.

Two Mohave Indian guides, Cairook and Ireteba, joined the Ives expedition, and the ship soon reached the head of navigation in Black Canyon, near the modern-day site of Hoover Dam. Turning the ship around, they rode the rapids to the end of Black Canyon, where they were met by a messenger from Fort Yuma carrying news of a packtrain of supplies bound for the ship. The packtrain soon arrived, and Lieutenant Ives and his men gluttonously devoured their fill and slept off the feast.

Satiated and rested, Lieutenant Ives sent the *Explorer* steaming south toward Fort Yuma, while he, Newberry, Egloffstein, and Mollhausen, as well as several crew members and numerous mules, followed the two Mohave guides out of Black Canyon. They hiked along a meandering course dictated by the location of springs, bound for Hualapai territory.

One of the Mohave guides, Ireteba, returned to their camp with two Hualapais who agreed to guide the party through Hualapai territory. A third Hualapai arrived the next morning, and the racist tendencies of Lieutenant Ives and his crew, not uncommon in their day, came spewing forth in describing the newcomer: "He had features like a toad's, and the most villainous countenance I ever saw on a human being," Lieutenant Ives wrote. "Mr. Mollhausen suggested that we should take him and preserve him in alcohol as a zoological specimen." Luckily, reason got the best of Lieutenant Ives and Mollhausen, and the plan to pickle a Hualapai was shelved. However, the disdain that Lieutenant Ives and his men felt toward Indians in general and the Hualapais in particular is repeated throughout Lieutenant Ives's official *Report*. The only exception to the offhand racist-presented-as-factual remarks about Indians was reserved for the Mohave guide Ireteba, who Lieutenant Ives and his men held in the highest regard.

Pushing northeast, the expedition gained elevation, walking into thicker and thicker stands of pinyon pine and juniper. Soon they arrived at a highpoint overlooking the Grand Canyon:

At the end of ten miles the ridge swell was attained, and a splendid panorama burst suddenly into view. In the foreground were low table-hills, intersected by numberless ravines; beyond these a lofty line of bluffs marked the edge of an immense canon; a wide gap was directly ahead, and through it were beheld, to the extreme limit of vision, vast plateaus, towering one above the other thousands of feet in the air, the long

*horizontal bands broken at intervals by wide and pro-
found abysses, and extending a hundred miles to the
north, till the deep azure faded into a light cerulean
tint that blended with the dome of the heavens. The
famous "Big cañon" was before us; and for a long time
we paused in wondering delight, surveying this stupendous formation through which the Colorado and its
tributaries break their way.*

Lieutenant Ives's "Big cañon" was the common name for the
gorge before John Wesley Powell bestowed the "Grand" moniker on
the canyon a little more than a decade later.

Lieutenant Ives wasn't satisfied with gaping at the glorious
scenery from above; he wanted to get down into the canyon. Accord-
ingly, they followed a side canyon into the Grand Canyon, reaching
the bottom at the confluence of Diamond Creek and the Colorado
River. As they descended, Lieutenant Ives got a little freaked out:

*The place grew wilder and grander. The sides of the
tortuous cañon became loftier, and before long we were
hemmed in by walls two thousand feet high. The
scenery much resembled that in the Black cañon,
excepting that the rapid descent, the increasing magni-
tude of the colossal piles that blocked the end of the
vista, and the corresponding depth and gloom of the
gaping chasms into which we were plunging, imparted
an unearthly character to a way that might have
resembled the portals of the infernal regions. Harsh
screams issuing from aerial recesses in the cañon sides*

and apparitions of goblin-like figures perched in the
rifts and hollows of the impending cliffs, gave an odd
reality to this impression.

Despite the ghoulish atmosphere, at least to Lieutenant Ives, they continued descending for 17 miles, not stopping until darkness forced them to. After they had set up camp, Ireteba told Lieutenant Ives that the Colorado River lay just ahead.

The next morning, April 5, 1858, they likely became the first party of whites to reach the bottom of the Grand Canyon. "A short walk down the bed of Diamond river . . . disclosed the famous Colorado cañon," Lieutenant Ives wrote in his *Report,* having regained his composure. "The scene was sufficiently grand to well repay for the labor of the descent."

Egloffstein, the topographer and artist, sketched the scene, as he had done at many scenic spots along their route. The resulting image of a dark and foreboding Inner Gorge, as well as several other sketches, illustrated Lieutenant Ives's 1861 *Report.*

From there, a new set of Hualapai guides led the Ives party back up Diamond Creek, and then up a side trail that proved quite difficult for the men and their mules. After becoming lost for a short time, the guides led the group to a small spring, where they spent the night.

The expedition continued east the next day, eventually arriving at the head of Hualapai Canyon on April 12. Then, as today, a trail leads down the canyon to a Havasupai settlement deep within the Grand Canyon, and Lieutenant Ives, several of his men, and some mules attempted the descent. They had to turn back, as it quickly became apparent that the mules couldn't negotiate the narrow trail. They were also suffering from nearly two days without water, and Lieutenant Ives sent them out of the canyon with one of the "Mexicans" in his crew, bound for "lagoons" some 30 miles away on the plateau.

On April 14, Lieutenant Ives and fifteen men descended the trail again. They came to a precipice, and after careful inspection of the area, Egloffstein discovered a ladder below the ledge they stood on. He bravely attempted to climb down the rickety ladder, but half of it split away under his weight. Somehow, he continued down the cliff face gripping the ladder rail that had held, but a few feet above the ground, the entire structure gave way, sending Egloffstein sprawling to the ground. A little banged up but otherwise okay, he set about exploring the canyon floor while his expedition mates tried to figure out how to retrieve him from the canyon. Lieutenant Ives wrote,

> *He found that he was at the edge of a stream, ten or fifteen yards wide, fringed with cottonwoods and willows. The walls of the cañon spread out a short distance, leaving room for a narrow belt of bottom land, on which were fields of corn and a few scattered huts.*

Although the group had little contact with the Havasupais living here, which they called the "Yampais," they had reached the Havasupai village, the first whites to visit the site since Padre Garcés in 1776. A Havasupai man accompanied Egloffstein back to the remains of the ladder, and Lieutenant Ives and his men lowered a "rope" made from tying the slings of their rifles together. "Whether it would support his weight was a matter of experiment," Lieutenant Ives wrote. The experiment was successful, and they soon started climbing out of the canyon.

From Hualapai Canyon, the Ives expedition continued east, running into trouble due to the lack of water in what Lieutenant Ives described as a "frightfully arid region." In describing this portion of the journey, Lieutenant Ives penned the words he is most famous for:

The region last explored is, of course, altogether value-less. It can be approached only from the south, and after entering it there is nothing to do but to leave. Ours has been the first, and will doubtless be the last, party of whites to visit this profitless locality. It seems intended by nature that the Colorado river, along the greater portion of its lonely and majestic way, shall be forever unvisited and undisturbed.

The last portion of the quote is usually left off, and Ives's remarks have come to be regarded as evidence of the shortsighted arrogance of the early explorers of the Grand Canyon region. Although he was off the mark, he was thinking of the land in terms of agriculture, town sites, and potential train routes, not in terms of a national park, a concept that didn't exist in Lieutenant Ives's day. Whatever the details, Lieutenant Ives very likely led the first party of whites to reach the bottom of the Grand Canyon, and what he saw knocked his socks off.

FIRST THROUGH THE GRAND CANYON?

- 1867 -

ON SEPTEMBER 7, 1867, A MAN WEARING NO PANTS arrived by raft at Callville, Nevada, on the Colorado River west of the Grand Canyon. However, his underclad lower half was not what stirred up a hubbub among the pioneer Mormons of the remote outpost, the ruins of which sit below the surface of Lake Mead today. The man had come downriver, floating by the Grand Wash Cliffs that mark the end of the Grand Canyon of the Colorado River. Seemingly, the only way this sunburnt, scraggly-haired man could have gotten to Callville was by floating through the Grand Canyon.

When the man was finally able to talk, he identified himself as a prospector by the name of James White. As the citizens of Callville crowded around to hear his tale, White told how he had been prospecting for gold along the San Juan River in southeastern Utah Territory, northeast of the Grand Canyon. White prospected with two men, Captain Charles Baker and George Strole, both of whom he had met in Fort Dodge, Kansas, where White had been living. As they worked their way down the banks of the San Juan, the canyon eventually narrowed, forcing the prospectors to strike out overland. Baker was convinced they could reach the Grand (as the Colorado River above its confluence with the Green was known then). They did indeed arrive at a river, and although they were able to make it down to the water on the talus southern slope, the sheer cliffs on the north side of the river ended hopes of traveling farther. Backtracking, the three prospectors, White said, were ambushed by Indians (probably Utes), and Captain Baker was shot dead. White and Strole escaped by scrambling back down to the river, building a makeshift raft, and setting themselves afloat. For supplies, they had only their guns, some rope, a hatchet, and several pounds of flour.

At first, the river they traveled on was calm, White told the gathered men. But soon the water became turbulent, and as the pair floated through the first rapids, Strole fell off the raft and drowned. In response to intense questioning by the crowd, all hungry for knowledge of the "Big Cañon," White told them he had been on the river for fourteen days, having rebuilt his raft several times after its repeated destruction in multiple rapids. He removed his pants to avoid being weighted down in the water during his repeated dunkings. The flour, his only food, was soon washed overboard. At first, he ate the rawhide scabbards of two knives, but thereafter, for seven days, White had nothing to eat. Eventually, White told the men, he came upon some Indians, who stole one of his pistols and his hatchet. But he was able to trade his other pistol for the hindquarters of a dog, which sustained him until he reached Callville. Given the condition of White when he arrived at Callville; the modest, straightforward manner in which he told his story; and the knowledge the townspeople had of the impenetrable canyon to the east, there was no doubt in Callville that James White was the first white man—and possibly the first man, period—to travel the length of the Grand Canyon on the Colorado River.

As White recovered in Callville over the following month, the story spread throughout the West. An article appeared in the (Prescott) *Arizona Miner* on September 14, under the headline "Navigation of the Big Cañon—A Terrible Voyage." White himself wrote a letter on September 26 to his brother in Kenosha, Wisconsin, detailing his experiences as best as he could, given his limited skills in translating his thoughts into writing. Despite nearly indecipherable grammar and a reliance on phonetic spelling, White imparted the basic facts of his journey and his sadness at the loss of his two fellow prospectors. This was to be the only written account of the journey White ever put on paper.

In January 1868 Dr. Charles Parry interviewed White on behalf of General William Palmer, a Civil War hero and prominent surveyor for western railroads. Parry recorded dates and distances, most likely inferring such specifics based on White's approximations. Parry noted White's description of the canyon, but by this time, four months after his arrival in Callville in a severe state, White's details varied greatly. Parry also recorded his belief that White and Strole had begun their journey upriver from the Green-Grand junction, near present-day Moab, Utah. Later, when powerful men discredited White, they seized on these details and the then-known realities of the Grand Canyon and Glen Canyon as proof that White was lying about his trip down the Colorado.

One year and nine months after James White arrived in Callville, Major John Wesley Powell and his crew of nine began their expedition of the Green and Colorado rivers, launching from Green River, Wyoming. It is unclear whether Powell knew of White's journey before he set out. But the issue of White came up during the congressional debate to fund Powell's expedition, and White is mentioned or alluded to in the journals of two members of Powell's crew, Jack Sumner and George Young Bradley. The crew made it through the Grand Canyon, arriving at the mouth of the Virgin River (today also beneath the waters of Lake Mead) in late August 1869. In mid-September, newspaper accounts of Powell's journey quoted the major as saying "the reported adventures of the man White . . . on the Grand Canyon of the Colorado, [are] a complete fiction." In addition to the adulation Powell and his crew received as the documented first expedition to travel through the Grand Canyon via the Colorado River, which provided motive to discredit White, the men found it impossible to believe a lone man could have made it through the treacherous rapids of the Colorado River on a driftwood raft. Followers of White's story now had a choice of believing the vague accounts of a semi-literate prospector or the opinion of Major John Wesley Powell, one of the great explorers of the American West, who would go on to publish *Exploration of the Colorado River of the West and Its Tributaries* (1875), his significantly enhanced account of the 1869 expedition. It was no contest; in the popular imagination, Powell was the first to travel the Colorado through the Grand Canyon.

In the years to come, further prominent writers discredited White, including the chronicler of the second Powell expedition down the Colorado (1871–1872), Frederick S. Dellenbaugh, who wrote: "Just where [White] entered the river is of course impossible to decide, but that he never came through the Grand Canyon is as certain as anything can be. His story reveals an absolute ignorance of the river and its walls throughout its whole course he pretended to traverse." Robert Brewster Stanton, who is credited as a member of the second and third expeditions down the Colorado River in the Grand Canyon (1889–1890), interviewed White about his journey. Stanton's posthumously published book *Colorado River Controversies* (1932), contains what Stanton calls the transcript of this 1907 discussion, but later historians—including Eilean Adams in her groundbreaking 2001 examination of White's journey, *Hell or High Water*—were able to document the highly questionable methods Stanton used to record and certify this "transcript." Despite this, Stanton used the transcript and his own knowledge of the treacherous Colorado River to discredit White in his book, asserting:

> *My trip from Green River, Utah, . . . to tide-water at*
> *[the Colorado River's] mouth on the Gulf of California*
> *. . . together with the subsequent years . . . which I*
> *spent upon the river and after years in painstaking*
> *research, gives me, I think, the right to speak with*
> *some authority.*

And so it went yet again: The assertions of a prominent and learned man "proved" White did not travel through the Grand Canyon. Stanton went so far as to claim that White had begun his journey a mere 60 miles above Callville, and traveled, somehow, overland from the San Juan River to the Grand Wash Cliffs, a distance of hundreds of miles over arid terrain around the Grand Canyon through hostile Hualapai territory. Even today some writers accept this logic-stretching theory as the gospel truth, or at least as cause to question White's veracity.

Whether James White traveled by raft through the entire Grand Canyon in 1867 may never be proven with certainty. He was not a man to promote his adventure, a fact that lends credence to the belief that he was telling the truth; in contrast, those with clear motives to disprove his story took full advantage of their bully pulpits to trash White. But it cannot be denied that the most reasonable explanation for White's arrival at Callville on September 7, 1867, is that he traveled down the Colorado through the Grand Canyon on a driftwood raft.

THE DEAD EXPLORERS

- 1869 -

MOST STUDENTS OF GRAND CANYON HISTORY are well acquainted with the 1869 expedition of John Wesley Powell and nine crew members down the Green and Colorado Rivers and through the Grand Canyon. Powell may well have been beaten to the feat by James White, but his group was undeniably the first expedition through the canyon and theirs was one of the great accomplishments in the exploration of the West. The Grand Canyon and the surrounding region were the "Great Unknown" in 1869, a vast area indicated on maps as "Unexplored." The significance of Powell's accomplishment is apparent today with even a cursory look at topographical maps of the Grand Canyon region: Lake Powell, Powell Plateau, Powell Point—the man's legacy is everywhere.

Powell Point, on Grand Canyon's South Rim, supports a monument to the 1869 crew and their heroic feat. However, three crew members' names are missing from the monument. William Dunn and brothers Oramel G. Howland and Seneca Howland left the expedition at Separation Rapid, a mere two days shy of the end of the Grand Canyon, and hiked out to the Arizona Strip on the northern side of the canyon. They never reached civilization, and speculation on what happened to the men has fueled a long controversy that continues today.

There is a lot of circumstantial and some concrete evidence that the Powell crew members were starting to get on each other's nerves by the time they reached Separation Rapid on August 27, 1869. The journals of two of the crew members indicate that Powell held Oramel Howland responsible for the loss of one of the expedition's boats, and that Powell had demanded reimbursement on the spot from William Dunn for a watch ruined when Dunn fell into the Colorado. Like an ignored hotspot in an ill-fitting hiking boot, the little indignities rubbed the men the wrong way and eventually became an open wound. When the crew reached the daunting cataracts of Separation Rapid, the Howlands and Dunn used the vicious rapid as their excuse to leave the expedition.

Despite some misgivings about the expedition's personnel, the Howlands and Dunn had good reason to fear Separation Rapid. As George Young Bradley, another member of the crew, wrote in his journal: "The water dashes against the left bank and then is thrown furiously back against the right. The billows are huge and I fear our boats could not ride them [even] if we could keep them off the rocks. The spectacle is appalling to us."

The night of August 27, the crew camped just above Separation Rapid. After dinner, Oramel Howland pulled Powell aside and told him that he did not think it was safe to run the rapid and that he, his brother, and Dunn would leave the river and hike out, regardless of what the rest of the crew did. Powell tried to persuade Howland to change his mind, but it was too late. The three would leave in the morning.

Powell surveyed the rest of the crew and found them game to continue on the river. He approached Oramel Howland one last time. Powell wrote: "We [had] another short talk about the morrow, and he lies down again; but for me there is no sleep. All night long I pace up and down a little path, on a few yards of sand beach, along by the river. Is it wise to go on?"

After a fitful night, Powell resolved to continue downriver. In the morning, the Howlands and Dunn took two rifles and a shotgun, some balls of dough, a watch that crewmember Jack Sumner asked them to deliver to his sister in case he perished, a letter from Powell to his wife Emma, and a duplicate copy of the trip's records. And then it was time to go. "It is rather a solemn parting;" Powell wrote, "each party thinks the other is taking the dangerous course."

As the two remaining boats of the expedition pushed out into the rapids, the Howlands and Dunn watched from a cliff that overlooked Separation. Surprisingly, the two boats were tossed around but made it through the rapids without loss of equipment, supplies, or lives. The crew fired their guns to signal their safe passage, but the three on shore waved them on.

Powell and his remaining crew pushed on, reaching the mouth of the Virgin River (today beneath Lake Mead), the end of the expedition, on August 30. Some of the crew continued on to Fort Yuma, but Powell and his brother Walter left the river and headed north to Salt Lake City. There, they received the news on September 15 that the Howlands and Dunn had been murdered, reportedly by Shivwits Indians angered over the men's alleged killing of a female Indian.

Powell was skeptical about the story, particularly the part about the men murdering an Indian woman. But nothing could be done about it at the time, and Powell hopped a train for Chicago.

But Powell did not let the matter drop. A year later he announced plans for a second expedition through the Grand Canyon, this time taking more time to create maps and collect data, and (hopefully) using less time worrying about survival—now that they knew the trip was possible.

To make the expedition easier, Powell decided to plant caches of supplies along the river so the next crew would not have to carry all of their supplies from the start. With this in mind, Powell traveled to the Arizona Strip, enlisting the assistance of Jacob Hamblin, a well-known Mormon explorer with close ties to Brigham Young, president of the Mormon Church. Hamblin knew the region and spoke the language of the Shivwits.

On September 19, 1870, a little more than a year after the Howlands and Dunn disappeared, Powell and Hamblin met with a group of Shivwits Indians near Mount Trumbull, just north of the Grand Canyon. At Powell's urging, Hamblin asked the Indians about the missing men. Powell recounted in his journal what Hamblin translated for him.

> *They [the Howlands and Dunn] came upon the*
> *Indian village starved and exhausted with fatigue.*
> *They were supplied food and put on their way to the*
> *[Mormon settlements in southern Utah]. Shortly after*
> *they left, an Indian from the east side of the Colorado*
> *arrived at their village and told them about a number*
> *of miners having killed a squaw in a drunken brawl,*
> *and [the Indians thought] no doubt these were the*
> *men; no person had ever come down the canyon; that*
> *was impossible; they [the Howlands and Dunn] were*
> *trying to hide their guilt. In this way [the Indian from*
> *the east] worked them into a great rage. They*

followed, surrounded the men in ambush, and filled
them full of arrows.

Powell accepted Hamblin's translation as fact, and he moved on to his further explorations of the region. The story Powell recorded became, more or less, the official explanation of the three explorers' disappearance.

It wasn't until 1979 that some started to publicly raise questions about the official story. Michael Belshaw, an author and historian, published an account of the affair in which he concluded that the Howlands and Dunn probably did not kill an Indian woman and more likely made it to the Arizona Strip in a weakened condition, where they were ambushed and killed by a Shivwits band.

Once the genie was let out of the bottle, the fate of the Howlands and Dunn became a large controversy that today remains unresolved. Historian Henry Dobyns and archaeologist and anthropologist Robert Euler, in response to Belshaw's essay, pointed out that it didn't make sense that the Indians told Powell of their involvement in the killings when they could have simply denied knowing anything about it. They also noted that the Shivwits had been allied with the Hualapai in their 1866–1869 war with the U.S. Army. Although the war had ended by September 1869, Dobyns and Euler surmised the Shivwits may not have known this and may have killed the men thinking they were soldiers.

These initial debates centered on "why" the men were killed. The debate would soon shift radically to "who" killed them. In 1993 retired biology professor Wesley Larsen discovered an intriguing letter in a trunk in an attic in Hurricane, Utah. The letter was written by Mormon William Leany to John Steele, another Mormon. In it, an agitated Leany cryptically accuses Steele of being "far from ignorant of those deeds of blood . . . [including] the day when those three were killed in our ward and the murderer killed to stop the shedding of more blood." Leany went on to refer again to the killing of three people in a room in their ward.

Larsen researched further, discovering no references or records of any trio, other than the Howlands and Dunn, being murdered in the region in the years before the letter was written in 1883. His research led him to conclude that the explorers had been killed by Mormons trying to protect John D. Lee, the accused ringleader of the 1857 Mountain Meadows Massacre (see the next chapter). Larsen believed the killer or killers thought the Howlands and Dunn were federal agents in search of Lee. They soon realized their error, and covered up the crime to avoid federal repercussions.

Larsen's research revealed a suspect in the killing: Eli N. Pace, a son-in-law of Lee. Pace died from a bullet to the head on January 29, 1870, just a few months after the Howlands and Dunn disappeared. Larsen surmised that Pace was "the murderer killed" in Leany's letter.

Larsen also pointed out that Jacob Hamblin was a devout Mormon with ties to the highest levels of the church, and he had ample motivation to "translate" for Powell inaccurate information if he knew Mormons were involved.

And still today the debate goes on. The bodies of Oramel Howland, Seneca Howland, and William Dunn have never been found. A plaque, posted in 1939, commemorates the spot at Separation Rapid where the Powell expedition went its separate ways.

THE FERRYMAN

- 1872 -

THE AMERICAN WEST IN THE 1870S WAS A WILD LAND: remote, sparsely populated, and a tad uncivilized from the viewpoint of many easterners. That suited the Mormons of Utah and northern Arizona just fine. Arriving in Utah Territory after being driven out of the Midwest by murderous mobs, the Latter-day Saints built a homeland in the wilderness. As time went on, the president of the church, Brigham Young, encouraged settlement in southern Nevada Territory, and northern Arizona Territory. From the southern Utah Territory town of Saint George, Mormons established settlements all over the region.

A few years earlier, in 1857, tensions between the Mormon Church and the federal government were high. In the late spring of that year, the federal government mobilized an army and sent them marching toward Utah Territory, in an effort to teach the independent-minded, polygamous Latter-day Saints a lesson about being a part of the United States. Word of the approaching troops enraged Utahans, and they prepared for war. The Paiute Indians of southern Utah Territory and the Arizona Strip (the portion of Arizona north of the Colorado River), who had experienced poor treatment at the hands of the federal government and of emigrants in wagon trains heading west (wagon train scouts often opened fire upon first sight of a Paiute, whether armed or not), also feared the approaching army and prepared to defend themselves.

In the late summer of 1857, the Fancher–Baker party, a wagon train of Arkansans and Missourians bound for California, made its way through the territory into the southwestern corner of Mormon country. Finding a fertile valley 35 miles southwest of the Mormon settlement of Cedar City, Utah Territory, the Fancher–Baker party set up camp in the valley known as Mountain Meadows. They planned to stay a few days, allowing their livestock to graze on the abundant vegetation.

Such an encroachment on their territory was unacceptable to the already angry Latter-day Saints, and local Mormon leaders resolved that the Fancher–Baker party would not leave the valley alive. Allied with the Paiutes, the Cedar City Mormons approached the wagon train encampment. The Paiutes attacked first, possibly at the urging of the Mormons, but the Fancher–Baker party quickly threw up their defenses and counterattacked, killing several Paiutes. After consultations with the Paiutes, a militia of fifty-four Mormons moved in on the valley. Major John D. Lee of the militia rode ahead into the Fancher–Baker camp, flying a truce flag. He proposed the group surrender their arms, allow those accused of killing Paiutes to be taken to Mormon jails, and turn their cattle over to the Paiutes. The Fancher–Baker party accepted the not-so-great offer, as they doubted their ability to fight their way out of Mountain Meadows. Surrendering their arms, the emigrants allowed the Mormons to separate them into groups of men, women and older children, and younger children—certainly a bad sign when viewed with the benefit of hindsight.

Once the group was neatly divided, the Mormons escorting the men suddenly turned on the emigrants and gunned them down. At the same time, Paiutes galloped in on the grouping of women and older children—and opened fire. Within a few minutes, what was to become known as the Mountain Meadows Massacre was over. That is all the time it took to kill every emigrant—more than 120 in all—except the youngest children, who now huddled in the back of a wagon, crying for their mothers.

When the slaughter was over, the hyped-up Mormons were horrified at what they had done. The militia quickly returned to Cedar City, and the men seeped back into Mormon society. Efforts by federal authorities to bring them to justice failed before a wall of silence.

In an effort to protect the Mormon Church from accusations of official involvement in the massacre, the president of the Southern Utah Mission, George A. Smith, held public fact-finding hearings. At one of those hearings, in the summer of 1858, a report was issued accusing "John D. Lee and a few other white men" of involvement in the massacre. Lee blended into society like the other militiamen, but the public accusation eventually focused demands for justice squarely on him. Over time he became the scapegoat for the collective Mormon guilt over Mountain Meadows.

In the fall of 1871, in an effort to distance the church from the tainted Lee, Brigham Young excommunicated Lee and ordered him to travel to the mouth of the Paria River on the Colorado. He was to establish a ferry, which would aid in the Mormon colonization of northeastern Arizona Territory. Lee unquestioningly followed Young's orders, and he departed for the Paria with one of his sons, two fellow Mormons, and fifty-seven head of cattle. He arrived at the mouth of the Paria on December 12, 1871. The rest of Lee's family, including two wives—Emma and Rachel—would soon join him in exile.

In January 1872, Lee ferried his first customers across the river, using an abandoned boat found near the crossing. The fifteen Navajos in the crossing party rode in the patched-up old boat, and Lee's Ferry was born. (The apostrophe is dropped in modern usage of the name: Lees Ferry.) Lee and his family spent most of 1872 developing their home site at Lees Ferry, the Lonely Dell Ranch. But he also ferried additional river crossers that year, using a stashed boat named the *Nellie Powell,* which belonged to the explorer Major John Wesley Powell.

By fall, the Mormon leaders in Salt Lake City feared further conflicts with the government over the denial of statehood for Utah, and they sought to establish a reliable, regular ferry not only to facilitate Mormon colonization of Arizona Territory but also to provide an escape route for southern Utah Mormons in the case of a federal invasion. Construction supplies began arriving in October, and the new ferryboat was ready for service by January 11, 1873. Over the spring, Mormon families poured into Lees Ferry as they attempted to settle in Navajo lands along the Little Colorado River, southeast—and on the other side of the Colorado—from Lees Ferry. According to his diary, Lee charged "75¢ for each Horse & $3 for each wagon" to ferry parties across.

The new boat lasted a mere six months, when a storm toppled a tree that bumped the boat out into the Colorado, where it was swept downstream never to be seen again. Around this time, Lee left Lees Ferry for Moenave, Arizona Territory, where he established a ranch; he fled because he feared a large contingent of U.S. Army soldiers was approaching the ferry. Meanwhile, Mormon boat builders fashioned a new ferryboat and launched it on October 15, 1873.

Lee held on for another year, but on November 7, 1874, he was arrested in Panguitch, Utah Territory, for his role in the Mountain Meadows Massacre. Lee was jailed until his trial in the summer of

1875, which resulted in a hung jury. Lee was put on trial a second time in the fall of 1876, and this time the jury convicted him and sentenced him to death. After his sentencing, Lee wrote in his diary, "My conscience is clear. I have not done anything with Evil intent. If I have Ered [*sic*] it is in Judgement [*sic*] & not of the Heart." On March 23, 1877, John D. Lee, sitting on his own coffin and blind-folded, was killed by firing squad in Mountain Meadows, the site of his crimes.

One of Lee's wives, Emma, stayed on at Lees Ferry after his death. The church appointed Warren M. Johnson to assist her after her husband's arrest, and Johnson ran the ferry after Emma left in 1879. In 1911 the Mormon Church sold the ferry to the Grand Canyon Cattle Company, which subsequently sold it to Coconino County. The county contracted a private company to run the ferry, and it remained in operation until 1928. The next year, the comple-tion of the nearby Navajo Bridge eliminated the need for the ferry.

Lees Ferry remains one of the most well-known spots in the inner canyon because of its modern-day status as the starting point for river trips heading down the upper portion of the Colorado River and the official starting point of Grand Canyon National Park. To river run-ners, Lees Ferry is Mile 0. Although no one crosses the Colorado at Lees Ferry anymore, the long-dead John D. Lee, a man who partici-pated in a horrific massacre but shouldered far more blame than his role called for, would likely be pleased so many boaters still launch from his Lonely Dell home.

THE CHASM OF THE COLORADO

- 1874 -

The whole gorge for miles lay beneath us and it was by far the most awfully grand and impressive scene [that] I have ever yet seen.

—THOMAS MORAN, IN A LETTER TO HIS WIFE,
AUGUST 13, 1873

BY THE TIME LANDSCAPE ARTIST THOMAS MORAN first looked out over the Grand Canyon from the North Rim at Toroweap in August 1873, he was already famous for his paintings and drawings of the American West. In 1870 *Scribner's Monthly* commissioned the thirty-three-year-old Moran to illustrate an article about Yellowstone, and the versatile artist created ink wash illustrations based on crude drawings of the wonders of Yellowstone sketched by two members of an expedition to the future national park in the summer of that year. The illustrations were published in the May and June 1871 issues of the magazine, along with the two-part article by Thomas Langford.

Buoyed by the publication of his Yellowstone sketches and armed with a recommendation from Jay Cooke (a Philadelphia banker and agent for the Northern Pacific Railroad), Moran talked his way onto the expedition of Dr. Ferdinand V. Hayden to Yellowstone in the summer of 1871. Relying on photographs taken by William Henry Jackson and his own sketches and watercolors made during the trip, Moran completed a 7- by 12-foot oil painting, *Grand Canyon of the Yellowstone.* Purchased by the government in 1872 for the then-momentous sum of $10,000, the painting was hung in the U.S. Capitol. Earlier that year, Congress had created Yellowstone National Park; congressional supporters of the Yellowstone bill had been heavily influenced by Moran's illustrations in *Scribner's,* as well as the sketches and watercolors he brought back from Wyoming after the Hayden expedition.

But when the famous explorer of the Southwest, Major John Wesley Powell, requested Moran's services for a trip to the Grand Canyon in 1872, the busy artist turned the major down: He had too many Yellowstone commissions to take time off that summer. A year later, after the artist had completed his work, he finally joined a new Powell expedition into the canyons of southwestern Utah Territory and on to the North Rim of the Grand Canyon.

Major Powell's theories on the formation of the Grand Canyon heavily influenced Moran. In 1875 the Government Printing Office published Powell's *Exploration of the Colorado River of the West and Its Tributaries,* including numerous illustrations by Moran. In that book Powell described the formation of the pinnacles and buttes of the inner canyon: "No human hand has placed a block in all those wonderful structures. The rain drops of unreckoned ages have cut them all from solid rock." Today, the effects of erosion on the formation of the canyon are widely known, but in 1875 many viewed Powell's ideas as radical. Regardless, Powell heavily influenced Moran, and the artist incorporated his idealized version of the role of falling water in the creation of the canyon in his equally large companion painting to the Yellowstone piece, *The Chasm of the Colorado,* completed in 1874.

The spectacle Moran created was of biblical proportions. In his rendering, a torrential downpour thunders across the inner canyon from the vantage point of the North Rim (Moran combined features seen from several North Rim viewpoints to create his painting). Sunlight highlights part of the painting and spotlights other features, while dark shadows on the rim and rock pinnacles surrounding the overlook frame the image. The view seems endless, fading into the misty skies on the distant horizon—perhaps 10 miles away or perhaps hundreds of miles across. A rattlesnake slithers through the boulders on the rim, while the tiny, silver Colorado River etches a route through the pinnacles near the center of the painting. Muted colors of gold, red, yellow, blue, green, purple, copper, and brown bring the painting to life, while moisture-laden clouds squeeze through the spires and buttes of the inner canyon. Two dried-out Douglas firs wilt on the desert's rim, while prickly pear cacti flourish among the boulders. Puddles from the sudden rainstorm wink from their catchments on the limestone surface. Powell, who loved the painting, later said of Moran's monumental work: "It displays the beauty of the truth."

The ominous painting is perhaps best described by its critics and champions. Richard Watson Gilder of *Scribner's Monthly* wrote:

> *It is awful. The spectator longs for rest, repose, and comfort. . . . The long vista of the distant table-land suggests a sunny place of refuge from all of this chaos*

and tumult. But for the rest there is only an oppressive
wildness that weighs down the senses. You perceive that
this terror has invaded the sky. Even the clouds do not
float; they smite the iron peaks below with thunderous
hand; they tear themselves over the sharp edges of the
heaven-defying summits, and so pour out their burdens
in showers of down-flying javelins.

Such vivid imagery accurately describes Moran's work, but also reflects the underlining awe Gilder held for the piece. Other critics missed Moran's creative intentions. Clarence Cook, writing in the *Atlantic Monthly,* compared the painting to Dante's descriptions of hell. But Cook, in the end, revealed his biases: "The only aim of art is to feed the sense of beauty; it has no right to meddle with horrors and desolation." Cook's viewpoint perhaps reflects less-than-modern thinking, as Vincent van Gogh and Pablo Picasso, men who painted some deeply disturbing masterpieces, would likely have argued. Art is about emotion, and *The Chasm of the Colorado* is both an amazing teaching tool and an expression of the monumental and fearsome forces that carved the canyon.

The painting likely reveals Moran's intense emotions about the Grand Canyon of the Colorado. Although he never returned to Yellowstone, he traveled back to the Grand Canyon many times during his career. In 1892 Moran agreed to paint a canvas for the Santa Fe Railway in exchange for free passage to the canyon (to Flagstaff by train and then overland by stagecoach to the canyon; the spur line to the South Rim had not yet been built). The Santa Fe used the resulting painting, *The Grand Colorado* (1892), in travel publications, and displayed the original at the newly constructed El Tovar Hotel on the South Rim after the hotel opened in 1905.

Moran made numerous additional trips to the canyon paid for at least partially by the Santa Fe. He returned to the canyon almost yearly after 1892 until his death in 1926. The railroad purchased many paintings and engravings from these trips, and also accepted additional works by the artist in exchange for railroad passage. With the Santa Fe's funds and the railroad's distribution of copies of the artist's work, Moran helped popularize the Grand Canyon in the minds of millions of Americans.

THE CRUEL COLORADO

- 1889 -

TODAY FEW END UP DEAD OR SEVERELY INJURED WHEN running the Colorado River through the Grand Canyon. Sure, going down the Colorado is not as safe as, say, reading a book—paper cuts and strained vision notwithstanding. But thousands of people run the Colorado every year nowadays, and the vast majority come bobbing along a week or two or so later, leaving the canyon with exhilarating memories but few lasting negative effects.

Robert Brewster Stanton and his crew suffered mightily in their first and second attempts at running the Colorado to the river's mouth at the Gulf of California in 1889–1890. An engineer by training, Stanton sought to survey the river to determine if a railroad could be built through the canyon. Although Stanton survived the two attempts and later wrote of the multiple disasters they faced in a matter-of-fact, unemotional style, his crew and his benefactor did not leave the canyon unscathed. Three did not leave the canyon at all.

In March 1889 Frank M. Brown, a wealthy Denver-based entre-
preneur, formed the Denver, Colorado Canyon and Pacific Railroad. He had no train engines, no tracks, no coal cars—but he had
a vision. Coal drove the steam engines that drove the economy of
Brown's day, and the western slope of the Rocky Mountains in Colorado had lots and lots of coal. Mountains and canyons stood
between those productive coal mines and the infant but growing
cities of Los Angeles and San Francisco, making the construction of
a railroad line through the canyon country to California highly
problematic. But when consulting a map of the region, one route
stood out: the Colorado River through the Grand Canyon. With a
relatively tame gradient (compared to going over mountains and in
and out of canyons) and a direct route (as perceived while standing
back a few feet from the map), the river canyon was the "perfect"
solution to his can't-get-the-lucrative-coal-to-the-people-who-will-
pay-big-money-for-it problem. Engineers had built railroads
through very difficult terrain, and the time-honored solution to
impassable mountains was to have the tracks follow river canyons.
To Brown, a railroad through the Grand Canyon was a no-brainer.
But first, the route needed to be surveyed.

Brown hired Stanton as the official surveyor of the river party,
and to help attract investors, Brown decided to lead the exploration
team himself to show how easy it was to go down the Colorado.
Brown personally planned the trip, ordering five lightweight, cedar,
narrow, short boats (the intention being to avoid the ponderous
portages Powell had faced with the weighty craft he employed) and
not ordering any life preservers for himself, Stanton, or the other
fourteen members of his crew.

When the crew loaded their boats at Green River, Utah Territory
(farther down the Green and wholly separate from Green River,
Wyoming, where the Powell expedition began), it quickly became

apparent that the boats were not big enough to carry all of the supplies. Thinking quickly, the team built a raft out of driftwood and loaded the remaining supplies onboard, to be towed behind the boat of George Gibson and Henry Richards, Stanton's servants. Seemed like a good idea at the time. They left Green River on May 25, 1889.

In Cataract Canyon in south-central Utah Territory, some 80 miles downriver from their starting point, the first rapid destroyed the raft and two of the crew's five boats. Supplies, cedar planks, and men spun and roller-coastered through the rapid; although all survived, the loss of the boats and most of their supplies crippled the expedition. And they hadn't even reached the Grand Canyon.

Stanton, four men, one boat, and some meager supplies (a few chunks of bread, coffee containing largely river water, some sugar, and a little condensed milk) stayed behind. They would work their way down the rapid, while Brown and the rest of the crew shot ahead to get supplies at Hite, or "Dandy Crossing," one of the mining camps in Glen Canyon. Drinking a lot of water to feel full, Stanton's men took six days to get through the 41 river miles of Cataract Canyon. As they emerged, weak and disgruntled, the crew met three men hauling supplies upriver for them. Temporarily rejuvenated, they pushed on to Dandy Crossing to meet Brown and his men.

Not surprisingly, three crew members quit the expedition at the mining camp, but Brown hired a mountain man, Harry McDonald, to shore up his disintegrating crew. Skilled at carpentry, the newest crewmember quickly got the party's remaining boats "riverworthy," and the crew pushed on to Lees Ferry in Arizona Territory. Thankfully, 150 miles of relatively tame water in Glen Canyon coddled the expedition, and they arrived at Lees Ferry on July 2, content and unscathed.

Brown rented a horse and rode 90 miles to Kanab, Utah Territory, to get supplies. He returned seven days later, and the expedition decided to push on with three overloaded boats and eight men (including Brown, Stanton, and the photographer Franklin A. Nims), the goal being to quickly get through Grand Canyon but not to survey the route: Nims's images would serve Brown's purposes of attracting investors.

The night of July 9, the expedition camped at Soap Creek Rapid, in Marble Canyon (today part of Grand Canyon National Park), 10 miles below Lees Ferry. The next morning, Brown confided in Stanton that he had dreamed about rapids for the first time since the trip began. This was probably of passing interest to Stanton at the time, but, within minutes of launching the boats, reality and Brown's inner dream world merged.

Brown's leading boat plunged into the tempest of Soap Creek Rapid. Stanton followed, but almost immediately hit big water only to see Brown's boatmate, Harry McDonald, waving frantically from shore. After running the rapid and pulling into an eddy, Stanton could hear McDonald, who shouted, "Brown is in there!" By "there" McDonald meant a whirlpool in the rapid. Looking back, Stanton saw nothing, except for Brown's notebook, floating in his direction. They scooped it out of the water, but Brown himself was never seen again.

The crew spent the day searching for Brown to no avail, and then set up camp for the night. Sad but not overly sentimental, the engineer Stanton wrote, "In this world we are left but little time to mourn." He and the remaining members of his team pushed off the next morning.

Over the next five days, they ran or portaged around twenty-four rapids. The twenty-fifth (ironically known today as 25-Mile Rapid) killed two more men, Peter Hansbrough and Henry Richards. Their boat became pinned under a low, overhanging ledge and overturned; both men drowned.

This was too much. As Stanton wrote, "Astonished and crushed by their loss, our force too small to portage our boats, and our boats entirely unfit for such work, I decided to abandon the trip." They camped one more night and cached supplies in a cave (today known as Stantons Cave) above the waterline, seeking shelter themselves as a storm rocked the canyon. It was not a pleasant night's sleep. "I have seen the lightning play," Stanton wrote, "and heard the thunder roll among the summit peaks of the Rocky Mountains, as I have stood on some rocky point far above the clouds, but nowhere has the awful grandeur equaled that night in the lonesome depths of what was to us death's cañon."

The next day they hiked out to the North Rim via South Canyon and eventually reached a Mormon cattle ranch. The settlers gave the beat-up explorers a wagon ride into Kanab, and Stanton was back in Denver in a few days' time. Immediately, he began planning a return trip.

On November 25, 1889, Stanton and his crew of eleven men (four returning from the previous year's disaster) pushed off from the mouth of Crescent Creek just above Dandy Crossing in Glen Canyon. Stanton had learned much from the year before, and he outfitted the expedition with longer, wider, deeper oak boats with sealed compartments to keep the boats afloat if they should capsize, cork life preservers for the crew, and watertight rubber bags for supplies.

When they reached Soap Creek Rapid where Brown had drowned, they were surprised to see how tame the river seemed, although they knew the river was 9 feet lower than it was during their last attempt. However, as Stanton would soon find out, big water wasn't the only danger on the Colorado.

On January 1, 1890, the photographer, Franklin Nims, fell from a cliff, plummeting 22 feet to the rocks below. He was alive, but quite beat up, including a broken leg just above the ankle. They spent the night nearby and pushed off the next morning, with Nims on a stretcher made of canvas drawn out between oars, to search for a way out of Marble Canyon and get the photographer some medical attention.

They found a route at Rider Canyon. Stanton and two men climbed out, and Stanton hiked 35 miles back to Lees Ferry to get help. The other men returned to the river to help bring Nims out. The next day the men began the ascent with Nims on the stretcher. At times, they hauled the photographer over scree slopes at an angle of forty-five degrees and up huge boulders blocking the route. They made it to the rim, but had not planned on spending the night, so they had brought few supplies. Soon it began to snow. They built a fire and fed their remaining provisions—a few pieces of chocolate dissolved in hot water—to Nims.

Stanton returned with a wagon the next morning, and Nims was taken back to Lees Ferry. Sixteen days later he reached Winslow, Arizona Territory, with a group of Mormons headed that way. A doctor there treated not only his broken leg, but several more broken or dislocated bones and a fracture at the base of his skull. Nims survived.

The eleven remaining men returned to the river and resumed the expedition. On January 17 they found the body of Peter Hansbrough, one of the crew members who had drowned on the previous expedition. They buried his remains the next morning. "The burial service was brief and simple," Stanton wrote. "We stood around the grave while one short prayer was offered, and we left him with a shaft of pure marble for his headstone, seven hundred feet high, with his name cut upon the base; and in honor of his memory we named a magnificent point opposite," today's Point Hansbrough.

Finally, mercifully, the tragedies came to an end. The rest of the trip was still rough but not deadly, although one crewmember, Harry McDonald, left the expedition and hiked out to the North Rim when he had had enough. Stanton and the remaining nine pushed on, eventually reaching Diamond Creek, where they could hike out and get provisions at Peach Springs, Arizona Territory. They took a break there and didn't launch again until late February. They reached the Sea of Cortez on April 26, 1890.

Ironically, although Stanton left the Colorado River with a firm conviction that a railroad could be built through the Grand Canyon, oil had since been discovered in California, and his backers refused to fund a railroad with the principal purpose of hauling coal.

EL TOVAR

- 1905 -

BEFORE THE TURN OF THE TWENTIETH CENTURY, getting to the Grand Canyon and staying at the rim was a bouncy, no-frills affair, with rustic accommodations greeting sore-bottomed tourists at the end of a long stagecoach, wagon, or horse ride. Few made the journey. The completion of a railroad spur line from Williams to Grand Canyon on September 17, 1901, opened the canyon to many more visitors, who could now glide to the canyon in relative comfort. It wasn't long before their stay at the canyon would rise to a high level of comfort and luxury as well.

Before the arrival of the railroad, visitors to the canyon more often than not ended up in the Grandview Point area, 13 miles east of today's Grand Canyon Village and then the location of the Grand View Hotel. Some also rode the stagecoach from Ash Fork to W. W. Bass's tourist operations, 25 miles west of the village. Train riders now arrived at the canyon a short distance from the rim in the heart of the tiny village, and small hotels and tent cabins sprouted to attend to the masses arriving daily.

The Santa Fe Pacific Railway, owner of the line to Grand Canyon, wanted a piece of this tourist-dollar pie. A big piece. Not long after the arrival of the railroad, the Santa Fe Pacific broke ground on a grand hotel, originally known as the Bright Angel Tavern, on the rim of what the railroad marketed as the "Titan of Chasms." During construction, the name of the hotel was changed to El Tovar, in honor of Pedro de Tovar, one of the explorers on Coronado's 1540 expedition to New Mexico and Arizona (although Tovar himself never came closer to the Grand Canyon than the Hopi pueblos). As was the case at many hotel and restaurant establishments along the Santa Fe Pacific line, El Tovar would be run by the Fred Harvey Company.

As construction progressed, the October 1, 1904, edition of the (Flagstaff) *Coconino Sun* gushed: "El Tovar will undoubtedly be one of the finest and most unique hotels in the southwest when completed, and its location a few steps from the brink of the stupendous canyon is unrivaled for scenic grandeur in the whole world." El Tovar opened to the public on January 14, 1905.

The architect was Charles F. Whittlesey, designer of several hotels along the Santa Fe Pacific line. Whittlesey envisioned a building that combined the styles of elegant Swiss mountain chateaus with rustic hunting lodges of the American West. Utilizing Oregon Douglas firs shipped in on the railroad and stone quarried locally, he designed the grandest of log cabins—an elegant, turreted hotel stretching to just a few yards shy of the rim. Petticoated and starched-collared visitors could look into the canyon from the gazeboed verandas on El Tovar's north end.

Guests entered El Tovar through a main sitting room, which featured exposed beams and rafters, a stone fireplace, Arts and Crafts–style furniture, and the mounted heads of several big game animals craning from the dark-stained, log walls. From the sitting room, visitors strolled into a two-story rotunda, anchored by a registration desk with wings of the hotel stretching to the north and south, and the main dining room to the west. The mezzanine lounge overlooking the registration area encircled an octagonal balcony and a grand-yet-rustic chandelier. Originally intended as a "ladies lounge," where women could "see without being seen—may chat and gossip—may sew and read—may do any of the inconsequent nothings which serve to pleasantly pass the time away," the lounge is also open today to men as well as women engaged in "consequential" pursuits.

The huge main dining room featured fireplaces opposing each other across the length of the room, like oversized, arching hockey goals set in stone. Large paintings by artist Brue Himeche depict some of the American Indian cultures with ties to the Grand Canyon, and picture windows on the northern end look out on the hotel's lawn and the canyon rim beyond. Harvey Girls, hospitable young women dressed like midwives (and contractually obligated to remain single) who worked at Fred Harvey Company restaurants throughout the West, served dinner guests. According to Christine Barnes, author of *El Tovar at Grand Canyon National Park* (2001), El Tovar "had its own bakery, butcher shop and bulk storage refrigerators to keep Pacific salmon, California fruit, Kansas beef and imported cheeses," unheard-of luxuries in the rural West of the early twentieth century.

El Tovar put many of the other hoteliers on the South Rim out of business, with the Grand View Hotel closing in 1908 and Cameron's Hotel becoming the village post office in 1910. The only survivor was the 1896 Bright Angel Hotel, which the Fred Harvey Company took over and reopened as Bright Angel Hotel and Camp after El Tovar was completed (Bright Angel Camp was replaced by the Mary Colter–designed Bright Angel Lodge in 1935).

Intended from the start to attract well-heeled tourists, El Tovar cost more than $250,000 to build—an enormous sum almost double the price to build Yellowstone's Old Faithful Inn, completed in 1904. El Tovar, originally with one hundred rooms, doubled the number of rooms available to visitors at the South Rim. In 1910, a new railway depot was completed at the base of the hill topped by El Tovar, providing visitors arriving by train a majestic first view of the hotel—with the canyon a teaser hidden beyond.

El Tovar is viewed by architectural historians as a transition building, bridging the gap between the Victorian past and the "National Park Rustic" style that came to dominate western national park buildings by the 1920s. The latter style emphasizes exposed beams and native stone, a look that blends with the natural surroundings. Many buildings at Grand Canyon built between 1914 and the 1940s evoke the National Park Rustic style.

Today, the hotel provides the favored accommodations of presidents and movie stars visiting the "Titan of Chasms." With the exception of some light fixtures, the addition of private bathrooms to the guestrooms, a marble-topped registration desk added during a 2005 renovation, modernized infrastructure, and a few other tweaks, the grandest of hotels at the Grand Canyon still looks much as it did in 1905.

GRAND CANYON MUMMIES

- 1909 -

IN 1909 THE START OF THE INTERNET AGE WAS still eighty-five or so years away. But the World Wide Web played a pivotal role in keeping alive a story that was published as fact in the (Phoenix) *Arizona Gazette* in 1909. The headline: "Explorations in Grand Canyon; Mysteries of Immense Rich Cavern Being Brought to Light; Jordan Is Enthused; Remarkable Find Indicates Ancient People Migrated from Orient." Scully and Mulder—or at least the *National Enquirer*—would have had a field day with this one.

Published on April 5, 1909, the article carries no byline and seems to rely almost exclusively on the comments of G. E. Kincaid, an explorer and prospector. The article begins by establishing that Kincaid was traveling down the Green and Colorado Rivers from Green River, Wyoming, to Yuma, Arizona. In the Grand Canyon, he and archaeologists from the "Smithsonian Institute" [*sic*] "made discoveries which almost conclusively prove that the race which inhabited this mysterious cavern, hewn of solid rock by human hands, was of oriental origin, possibly from Egypt, tracing back to Ramses. If their theories are borne out by the translation of the tablets engraved with hieroglyphics, the mystery of the prehistoric people of North America, their ancient arts, who they were and whence they came, will be solved. Egypt and the Nile, Arizona and the Colorado will be linked by a historical chain running back to ages which staggers the wildest fancy of the fictionist."

Well, now. That would be an interesting twist on all we know, even nearly a century after the article was published. Luckily, the article gets much more specific, describing a mile-long tunnel to a huge chamber with "scores of passageways [radiating] like spokes of a wheel." The complex, according to the article, includes hundreds of rooms, a cross-legged idol carving that "almost resembles Buddha" surrounded by smaller carvings, "some very beautiful in form—others crooked-necked and distorted shapes," urns, cups of copper and gold, seed-filled granaries, and hieroglyphics everywhere you looked. Arguably the most interesting find, according to the article, was a crypt with "tiers of mummies, each one occupying a separate hewn shelf. . . . Some of the mummies are covered with clay, and all are wrapped in a bark fabric." To give you an idea of the size of the cave complex, the article continues, "Upwards of 50,000 people could have lived in the caverns comfortably."

Kincaid is quoted in the article as detecting a "snaky smell" when approaching one chamber. "Our light would not penetrate the gloom," he told the newspaper, "and until stronger ones are available we will not know what the chamber contains. Some say snakes, but other[s] boo-hoo this idea and think it may contain a deadly gas or chemicals used by the ancients. No sounds are heard, but it smells snaky just the same. The whole underground installation gives one of shaky nerves the creeps."

According to the article, the exploration of the caverns was under the direction of Professor S. A. Jordan of the "Smithsonian Institute" [*sic*]. The article described him as "prosecuting the most thorough explorations, which will be continued until the last link in the chain is forged."

Interestingly, the newspaper ran two stories on G. E. Kincaid, adventurer and prospector. The first predated the astounding April 5 story by a few weeks. On March 12, 1909, the *Arizona Gazette* ran a short piece:

G.E. KINCAID REACHES YUMA

G.E. Kincaid of Lewiston, Idaho, arrived in Yuma [Arizona] after a trip from Green River, Wyoming, down the entire course of the Colorado river. He is the second man to make this journey and came alone in a small skiff, stopping at his pleasure to investigate the surrounding country. He left Green River in October, having a small covered boat with oars, and carrying a fine camera, with which he secured over seven hundred views of the river and canyons which are unsurpassed. Mr. Kincaid says one of the most interesting features of the trip was passing through the sluiceways at Laguna dam [just north of Yuma]. He made this perilous passage with only the loss of an oar.

Some interesting archaeological discoveries were unearthed and altogether the trip was of such interest that he will repeat it next winter, in the company of friends.

The truly remarkable thing noted in this piece is the fact that G. E. Kincaid is credited as the second person to travel nearly the entire length of the Green and Colorado Rivers between Green River, Wyoming, and Yuma, Arizona, after John Wesley Powell—although Powell himself left the river at the confluence with the Virgin River (today under Lake Mead), and some of his men continued on to Yuma. This would indeed be true if Kincaid's story is true. There had been scant few expeditions on the Colorado in Grand Canyon since Powell's first in 1869 (Robert Brewster Stanton et al., in 1889 and 1890; George Flavell and Ramon Montez in 1896; Nathaniel Galloway and William Richmond in 1897; "Hum" Woolley, John King, and Arthur Sanger in 1903; Nathaniel Galloway and Julius Stone in 1907; and Charles Russell and Edwin Monett in 1907) and no solo trips, other than James White's disputed 1867 raft trip through the canyon. If G. E. Kincaid traveled nearly the full length of the Green and Colorado Rivers in 1908, "stopping at his pleasure to investigate the surrounding country" (acting as a tourist, in other words), by himself, it would have been very big news across the country. However, as far as can be ascertained, two articles published in the *Arizona Gazette* are the only ones of the era discussing Kincaid's finds.

Modern-day chroniclers of Colorado River runners, including Bonnie Brune and Brad Dimock, both writing in *A Gathering of Grand Canyon Historians: Ideas, Arguments, and First-Person Accounts* (2005), make no mention of the Kincaid trip, although both authors exhaustively mention every other early river trip. Historian David Lavender likewise makes no mention of Kincaid's first-of-its-kind solo river trip down the Green and Colorado Rivers in his book *River Runners of the Grand Canyon* (1985).

Also of interest in this initial article is the fact that Kincaid said the most exciting thing about the trip was the slip and slide through the sluiceways at Laguna Dam, and only passing mention is made to "archaeological discoveries." One could argue that Kincaid wanted to keep a lid on what he had seen until he contacted the Smithsonian Institution, which is what he apparently did shortly after completing his trip. But not mentioning the "lost civilization" Kincaid supposedly found in a cave in Grand Canyon is a curious omission nonetheless.

Today, a small contingent of devoted online amateur Canyonophiles/Egyptologists have kept alive the odd *Arizona Gazette* story and even gone so far as to accuse the Smithsonian Institution and the National Park Service of a vast cover-up of an ancient Egyptian society in the Grand Canyon. Such writers point out that the Smithsonian Institution denies any knowledge of G. E. Kincaid, Professor Jordan, or Egyptian artifacts in the Grand Canyon as evidence of a cover-up. They also point out that the National Park Service does not allow inner-canyon hikers to enter caves, except for the well-known Cave of the Domes below Horseshoe Mesa.

In both cases, these researchers are correct. The Smithsonian does say it has no knowledge of the Kincaid/Jordan find or of the men themselves. That in itself is not evidence of a cover-up, however, as it may just indicate that the whole thing is a hoax. It is also true that the park service does not allow inner-canyon hikers to enter caves unless they have a research permit. This may be in order to hide the existence of the remains of a vast, underground society of Egyptians (or perhaps of some other far-from-home canyon residents from lands further to the east, given the reported existence of a Buddha-like statue), or it may be in order to protect the safety of Grand Canyon visitors and to protect artifacts that may be in the caves, such as the split-twig figurines found in Stantons Cave in 1934. (As of this writing, the National Park Service is reviewing its cave policies and is considering allowing wider access to the park's many caves.)

Some writers have suspected that if the underlying story Kincaid told to the *Arizona Gazette* is true, he may have been looking at remains of an ancestral Puebloan culture. Artifacts from these peoples as well as earlier and later occupants of the canyon have been found throughout the park.

The facts that no newspaper other than the *Arizona Gazette* picked up the story, that G. E. Kincaid and Professor S. A. Jordan do not seem to have existed, and that there are no records of any excavation of a site of this nature in the Grand Canyon at the time the article ran suggests this is a rumor kept alive by this age of anyone with an Internet connection having the ability to publish their opinions. But maybe, just maybe, in a cave deep in the Grand Canyon, Buddha awaits.

Note: As discussed, it is illegal to enter caves in the Grand Canyon without a permit at this time. It has been and always will be illegal to remove any artifacts from Grand Canyon National Park, whether potsherds, historical mining equipment, or clay-covered, bark-wrapped mummies.

MOVING PHOTOGRAPHY

- 1911–1912 -

IN THE EARLY YEARS OF THE TWENTIETH CENTURY, still photography was a cumbersome process and motion picture photography was almost unheard of. Ellsworth and Emery Kolb, pioneer photographers at the Grand Canyon, had built Kolb Studio at the Bright Angel trailhead as a home, store, and vantage point to take photographs of "dudes" (mule-riding tourists) headed down the Bright Angel Trail atop a long-eared steed. Later the building would be expanded to include a darkroom and an auditorium.

Ellsworth was the more adventurous of the brothers, and Emery gave him credit for first coming up with the idea to boat down the Green and Colorado Rivers from Green River, Wyoming, to Needles, California, and to film sections of the trip on a newfangled motion-picture camera. If successful, they would be the second boat party (after Major Powell in 1869) to travel from the Wyoming outpost through the Grand Canyon on the Green and Colorado.

Although the Kolb brothers had lugged heavy plate cameras all over the Grand Canyon and were well known for climbing to precarious spots to get just the right photograph, they had never even seen a motion-picture camera, much less used one. And their Colorado River running experience consisted of a single fishing trip by Emery in 1904, which ended with a sunken boat and Emery trapped on a rock in the middle of the river. Ellsworth had to hike down the Bright Angel Trail with a life preserver and a rope to rescue his marooned brother.

Nevertheless, the brothers began to contemplate a Powell-like river trip as early as 1906, and by the spring of 1911, they began preparations for the run, with a goal of launching the trip in the fall. They ordered boats from the Racine Boat Company in Wisconsin, following designs used by Julius Stone and Nathaniel Galloway during their 1907 run of the Grand Canyon. They searched far and wide for a motion-picture camera, but soon discovered that it was almost impossible to acquire one. By luck, the Kolb brothers connected with Frederick I. Monsen of New York City, who sold the brothers one of his two motion-picture cameras for the sum of $250. Ellsworth headed east to secure the camera, to buy film plates for the two still cameras they planned to bring, and to get his hands on as much motion-picture film as he could find. The movie film proved nearly as difficult to acquire as the camera.

Early in the planning stages, the Kolbs recognized a need to secure the services of a third man on their trip. With two boats and a desire to film the trip, someone was needed to either run one of the boats or to operate the motion-picture camera from shore. Finding no acceptable takers at Grand Canyon, they advertised the "job opening" in a San Francisco newspaper. James Fagan, recommended to the Kolbs by another man who had to back out of the trip, eventually signed on.

The Kolbs rendezvoused in Denver on August 30, 1911, acquiring additional supplies needed for the trip. They arrived at Green

River, Wyoming, on September 2. Things were delayed a few days as they waited for confirmation that the boat company had received payment for the boats. They also were awaiting the arrival of Fagan, who was en route to Green River from San Francisco. In a letter to his wife Blanche written on September 5, Emery noted that they didn't want to start their trip if the light was not good, because they wanted to film their launch. As the weather was cold and stormy in Green River at the time, they may have delayed a day or two to get the shot.

The Kolbs set up a floating tent darkroom in one of the boats to develop photographic plates while on the river. Fagan arrived on September 6, and the brothers soon received word that their account was settled with the boat company.

One of the Kolb brothers wrote a letter to the (Flagstaff) *Coconino Sun,* dated September 2 but published the day the three men launched at Green River. The writer notes that "the town people here look on us as a physician might a hopeless case and then relate weird stories of others who attempted the voyage and were never heard from again." The letter was signed simply "Kolb Bros."

On the chilly morning of September 8, the three men launched onto the Green, which was running low. The low water level caused problems early in the trip, as the boats repeatedly became stuck on sandbars. Ellsworth, Emery, and Fagan all spent a good amount of time wading, pushing the boat along.

At first, Fagan seemed to fit right in. Emery wrote Blanche that, "Jimmie Fagan . . . is certainly the man. . . . He neither drinks nor uses tobacco and the greatest trouble [is that] he wants to do everything himself. He is certainly ok and says he will stick as long as we do." Fagan filmed the brothers running rapids and gamely got flipped into the river several times, but always came up grinning. At first.

But by the time the three crossed back into northeastern Utah from Colorado (the Green River meanders from Utah into Colorado and back again into Utah at this point), the Kolb brothers began to fear for Fagan's sanity. He seemed surly and depressed, and by the time they reached a ranch near Vernal, Utah, he begged the brothers to let him out of the trip. Feeling more confident of their river-running abilities and having come to the conclusion that Fagan was now more of a hindrance than a help, the Kolbs dropped Fagan off at the ranch, and he headed home to San Francisco.

As it turned out, the Kolbs did not have time on their trip to develop the motion-picture film or photographic plates they brought along. They sent the film and plates on ahead, first to Green River, Utah, where they expected a layover with time to develop the film and plates, and later to the South Rim to await their return. They also sent four rolls of movie film that had been drenched to Rochester, New York, home of Eastman-Kodak, to see if the images could be saved.

After the predicted layover in Green River, Utah, the Kolbs pushed on, reaching Lees Ferry at the start of Marble Canyon (today the eastern section of Grand Canyon National Park) on November 7. The brothers had read all the available books on the Colorado River, and they knew they would reach Soap Creek Rapid shortly after leaving Lees Ferry, and that Frank Brown had drowned below that rapid during the first Stanton expedition in 1889. According to William C. Suran, author and editor of *The Brave Ones: The Journals and Letters of the 1911–1912 Expedition down the Green and Colorado Rivers by Ellsworth L. and Emery C. Kolb* (2003), the Kolb brothers "took extra precaution before leaving Lees Ferry," including making sure that the film was protected from water damage by applying paraffin, that any leaks in the boats were caulked, and that all loose objects in the boats were stuffed into compartments. The only thing they couldn't fully protect was themselves. On November 18 the brothers left Lees Ferry.

Unintimidated by Soap Creek Rapid, Ellsworth prepared to run the white water as Emery ran the motion-picture camera downriver. Ellsworth was to provide some great footage, as a particularly nasty cataract flipped his boat, sending him flying into the Colorado. He managed to right the flooded boat and continue to the base of the rapid, where Emery helped unload everything and lay it out on the beach to dry.

Perhaps the rapid stoked competitive fire in Ellsworth, but for whatever reason, he insisted on running Emery's boat through the rapid, even though it was now dusk. Again the boat flipped, and Ellsworth ran the rapid once again hanging onto the swamped boat. Emery could barely make out the overturned hull in the twilight, but he acted quickly nevertheless, rowing out to rescue his brother and his boat.

The motion-picture camera was to survive several dunkings in the river during the Kolbs' trip, and each time it had to be dismantled so the numerous moving parts could dry out. Giving a plug for the reliability of old-fashioned mechanical photographic equipment, the brothers were always able to dry out the camera and get it running again.

On November 16 the Kolb brothers reached Rust's Camp (today the site of Phantom Ranch, built eleven years later), and the next day they hiked to the South Rim on the Bright Angel Trail. As Emery was to find out, his wife Blanche had been very sick as well as pregnant while the brothers were on the river. Upon his arrival at the rim, he, Blanche, and their daughter Edith boarded the next train to Williams, transferring there to a train bound for Los Angeles, where Blanche could receive medical treatment. Sadly, Blanche miscarried. Emery stayed with his wife and daughter until Blanche was out of danger and in the care of a nurse; he returned to the canyon only after Blanche insisted.

Hiking through heavy snow leading pack mules, the brothers, a third Kolb brother named Ernest, and local stagecoach driver Bert Lauzon, who talked the brothers into letting him assist them on the remainder of their journey, headed for the foot of the Bright Angel Trail. Ernest Kolb would ride with the three as far as the South Bass Trail, where he would have to hike out to the South Rim to tend to the Kolbs' business during their absence.

The four made a good team; as Suran noted in his book, "Bert would position himself near the bottom of the cataract with a rope and life preserver in case of an accident, while Ernest operated the camera, taking pictures of his brothers making the run. The boats dipped up and down in the waves and were out of sight frequently, offering some good action on film."

On December 22 Ernest hiked out on the South Bass Trail, and Christmas Day found the remaining three repairing a man-sized hole in Emery's boat. Vicious rapids lay ahead, including Lava Falls and Separation Rapid, but the Kolbs and Lauzon made it through, traveling through a Hoover Dam–less Black Canyon and reaching Needles on January 18, 1912—101 days after leaving Green River, Wyoming.

The film the brothers put together from their adventure was a runaway hit—but not at the Grand Canyon. The Kolbs were forced to take the film on tour when the U.S. Forest Service, which then oversaw the canyon, would not allow the Kolbs to show it at the South Rim. The Kolbs, particularly Emery, had irritated both the forest service and the Fred Harvey Company, the dominant concessioner at the South Rim, and the banning of the film was probably a reflection of those hard feelings.

However, the Kolb film tour was wildly successful. They ran the film at packed houses all over the eastern half of the country, including at the National Geographic Society in Washington, D.C. Meanwhile, Ellsworth wrote a book about the trip, *Through the Grand Canyon from Wyoming to Mexico* (1914), and the Kolbs worked to gain the permission of Ralph Cameron, who controlled a mining claim for the land Kolb Studio was built on, to make an addition to the building of an auditorium to show the film. As the addition would be on a privately held mining claim, the Kolbs did not need the permission of the forest service. The addition was completed in the spring of 1915, and the Kolbs began showing their film. The movie would run continuously at the South Rim until Emery Kolb's death at the age of ninety-five in 1976.

DRIVING TO THE COLORADO RIVER

- 1914 -

IN 1914 L. WING OF THE METZ AGENCY IN LOS ANGELES and reporter O. K. Parker embarked on a grand publicity stunt to drive from Los Angeles to the bottom of the Grand Canyon. Their mode of transportation was a Metz roadster: a bucket-seated, twenty-two-horsepower demon that looked kind of like a Chitty-Chitty-Bang-Bang go-kart with bicycle tires. From L.A. they crossed the Mojave Desert, no trifling feat in itself, and drove on to Grand Canyon Village on the South Rim. They used the scenic opportunity to photograph the Metz roadster poised at the rim, including a now-famous photo of one of the adventurers peering over the edge, the roadster backlit just behind him. As O. K. Parker wrote in his article about the trip, "It took a lot of grit to drive the car right towards that fearful plunge, but Mr. Wing, who handled the wheel, had every confidence in the car and its control, and did not put on the brakes until the front wheels were right at the very edge of the precipice." The drivers camped overnight at the village and drove on to Peach Springs on the Hualapai Indian Reservation the next morning.

Peach Springs was to be the starting point of their excursion.

At the time, there was no automotive road to the Colorado from Peach Springs. Recognizing that they might not make it back out of the canyon with a working roadster, the two arranged with the Hualapais to have two horses carrying extra rations on standby, ready to be led into the canyon in case the motorists didn't return to Peach Springs in forty-eight hours.

Off they went, bouncing along down a gorge at the beginning of their mile-deep descent, over 21 miles of boulder-strewn terrain. Parker noted that sometimes the canyon they were descending narrowed so severely that they could not get the car through. They were then forced to back up until they could find a place to drive up out of the bed of the wash and around the bottleneck. Parker, who noted in his article that he was writing for drivers or those considering buying an automobile, praised the Metz, "In places the grade was 25 to 30 percent, and only the remarkable pulling qualities of the fiber grip transmission enabled us to get over the terrific deposits of debris and boulders that mark the accumulation of ages." Although General Motors or Toyota today may not be impressed by a "fiber grip transmission," they likely would recognize Parker's copywriting talent—and appreciate the free advertising. The reporter was clearly trying to tell us that the Metz roadster was one hell of a car.

The Metz climbed over boulders a foot and a half to three feet high, impressive even to modern-day SUV drivers. "The twisting and straining of the axles, springs and frame of the car," Parker wrote, "was almost beyond the endurance of steel. For an example of extreme flexibility, one can hardly equal it." Although reading Parker's story about the trip often feels like reading corporate ad copy, absorbing his description of the trip and the way the Metz roadster handled obstacles slowly changes your mindset: The car's ability to handle some truly rugged terrain was amazing.

On that first day, they made it within a mile and a half of the Colorado River before pulling over to camp for the night. A rainy night soaked the drivers, but they maintained their enthusiasm and were up at daybreak to renew their trip.

On this day, they emerged from the gorge they had been descending from Peach Springs and met up with Diamond Creek; the flowing water created a new obstacle for the indestructible Metz: quicksand! But the roadster was able to muster every one of its twenty-two horses to rush across multiple slurries of water and silt. The Metz, somehow, didn't sink.

They soon encountered gigantic boulders much larger than the car itself. They couldn't drive over or around these monstrosities. However, they were able to pile smaller rocks and brush high enough to make a ramp for the roadster to ascend and descend, and the Metz drove on.

Around 11:00 A.M. on the second day of driving, L. Wing and O. K. Parker parked the Metz with the wheels just touching the steadily flowing Colorado. Wasting no time admiring the river, the two turned around and began the return trip, this time much more confident that they would easily make it back in, as Parker noted, "remarkable time."

"Now," Parker wrote, "instead of being experimenters, so to speak, we were tourists, and I can assure you we keenly enjoyed the exhilarating trip to the top, and it was with no little satisfaction that we looked back from each new height gained with the thought that we were probably the first to make the trip in this way." (They were indeed the first to drive to the Colorado River in the Grand Canyon.)

Today, an automotive road descends the Metz-trailblazed route from Peach Springs to the Diamond Creek confluence with the Colorado, making access in a Buick or a Honda or a Volkswagen a piece of cake. But in 1914, if you wanted to drive from L.A. to the Colorado River, you better have been behind the wheel of a Metz.

PHANTOM RANCH

- 1922 -

TOWERING WALLS OF SCHIST AND GRANITE REACH SKYWARD from the bottom of the Grand Canyon at Bright Angel Creek. When standing on the Silver Bridge in the Inner Gorge, the rims of the canyon proper are not visible: The gorge walls, some as high as 1,400 feet and nearly vertical, block the view back to the top. At an elevation of 2,400 feet above sea level, the area around Bright Angel Creek at its confluence with the Colorado River runs as much as twenty-five degrees hotter than the 7,000-foot-high South Rim. In the summertime, the difference is balmy shirtsleeve weather in the piñon-juniper forest of the South Rim and can't-be-outside-a-second-longer-or-I'm-going-to-go-bonkers heat at the canyon floor. In this dry sauna, just up Bright Angel Creek from its confluence with the Colorado, Santa Fe Railway architect Mary E. J. Colter designed—and the Fred Harvey Company built—Phantom Ranch, a seemingly improbable oasis a mile below the rims of the Grand Canyon.

But Colter and the Fred Harvey Company weren't the first to think of the Phantom Ranch area as a place of solace and rejuvenation.

In 1869 John Wesley Powell and his men came upon Bright Angel Creek and liked what they saw. Powell wrote: "Early in the afternoon we discover a stream entering from the north—a clear, beautiful creek, coming down through a gorgeous red canyon. We land and camp on a sand beach above its mouth, under a great, overspreading tree. . . ." Powell and his men liked the spot so much they spent a layover day along the creek. Although Powell initially named the stream "Silver Creek," by the time he published his report on his two river trips down the Colorado in 1875, he changed the name to the more evocative Bright Angel Creek.

By 1906 David Rust had established a camp just downcreek from Phantom Ranch's future site. A not-so-modest man lacking a creative streak, Rust named his accommodations "Rust's Camp." In 1907, to increase tourist traffic, he strung a cable across the Colorado that was capable of carrying a man and his mule. With the improvements Rust made to the North Kaibab Trail (then known as the Bright Angel Trail, an extension of the trail by the same name on the south side of the river), tourists could now travel from rim to rim through the corridor, stopping to rest at Rust's Camp along the way.

In 1913 former president Theodore Roosevelt spent the night at Rust's Camp; he was en route to the North Rim to hunt mountain lions with James T. "Uncle Jim" Owens, the game warden for the Kaibab National Forest. Thereafter, the site was known as "Roosevelt's Camp," at least until Phantom Ranch was built nine years later. Phantom Ranch itself is named after Phantom Canyon, a side canyon upstream from the tourist camp.

In 1921 the wood-and-rope Kaibab Suspension Bridge replaced the old cable crossing. At 420 feet long and quite wiggly, the new bridge was not for the faint of heart. But both hikers and mules could now cross the Colorado relatively quickly, making a serious tourist camp at Phantom Ranch much more practical.

Colter transferred some of her designs for the cabins and main canteen at Phantom Ranch from an earlier project that had been planned for Indian Garden, 4.5 miles up the Bright Angel Trail from Phantom Ranch. Indian Garden, which is also just over 4.5 miles from the South Rim, has a similar, clear-running stream—Garden Creek—but sits at a higher elevation, allowing for cooler year-round temperatures. This was the originally envisioned site for Fred Harvey's inner-canyon oasis in the Corridor area (at the time, the company also had canyon accommodations in the form of tent-cabins at Hermit Camp, about 15 miles west of Indian Garden). It may have been World War I that put the kibosh on the Indian Garden ranch idea, or it may have been the ongoing battle with Ralph Cameron over control of the Bright Angel Trail, the only direct route to Indian Garden. Regardless, many of Colter's Indian Garden designs were incorporated and adapted to Phantom Ranch.

Although Phantom Ranch was not intended to be and has never served as a working ranch, Colter designed it based on western ranches she had visited, with a central dining hall surrounded by four guest cabins. As she did with most of her structures on the South Rim, such as Hopi House and Hermits Rest, Colter designed Phantom Ranch so it would blend in with the spectacular surroundings rather than compete with them. She incorporated locally found, uncut stone in her designs and scattered the guest cabins unevenly to give Phantom Ranch a more relaxed feel. The bungalow cabins were simply decorated, with beds, a desk and chair, and a Navajo rug covering the floor. Meals were to be taken at the dining hall. With the exception of the stones, all construction materials and, later, all supplies for the accommodations, had to be brought down by mule. Today that tradition continues, and mules also carry all trash back to the rim for disposal. Colter and her sister, Harriet, journeyed to Phantom Ranch by mule for the grand opening on November 9, 1922, a merciful time of year to visit the Inner Gorge.

Over the years, Phantom Ranch grew and new amenities were added. In 1925 the National Park Service completed the South Kaibab Trail, cutting 2 miles off the 9-mile hike from the South Rim to Phantom Ranch. In 1926 a generator brought electricity to the ranch, and in 1928 Colter designed an additional eight guest cabins and a recreation hall, which joined the dining hall orbit. That same year, the steel, much more stable Black Bridge replaced the 1921 Kaibab Bridge. The Civilian Conservation Corps built a pool in 1934 (the pool was filled in and buried in 1972), and they connected the Bright Angel Trail to the South Kaibab Trail in 1936, via the precipitous River Trail carved into the schist and granite of the Inner Gorge. As the cottonwoods—planted when Phantom Ranch was originally constructed—grew tall, the ranch became a shady, creekside spot that has seemed like nirvana to countless hikers and mule riders over the years.

Originally, Phantom Ranch was a rather exclusive spot, catering to a select clientele who could afford to travel there by mule. Today it still offers some of the priciest accommodations at Grand Canyon, and most who stay in the cabins still get there by mule, but the addition of a bunkhouse and the location of Bright Angel Campground between Phantom Ranch and the Colorado River bring many less-well-off hikers to the site to sit in the air-conditioned lodge and to scarf down steak, stew, ice water—and ice-cold beer.

Although the hearty eats and refreshing drinks would have been welcome in John Wesley Powell's day, then as now Phantom Ranch rewards those willing to make the effort to get there. It is a spectacular place like no other spot in the world.

INNER CANYON LANDING

- 1922 -

IN 1922 MOST PILOTS THOUGHT IT WAS IMPOSSIBLE to fly over—much less land within—the Grand Canyon. Even today, it seems like a harebrained—not to mention illegal—plan. At the time, many believed that the jagged topography and the unpredictable updrafts would surely take the controls away from any barnstormer dim enough to give a landing a try, sending him spiraling to his death.

A. Gaylord, writing in his 1922 piece "Into the Grand Canyon and Out Again by Airplane" in the *Literary Digest*, emphasized the thinking of the day:

> *[In 1921] a commander of the British Royal Flying*
> *Corps visited the Grand Canyon . . . and gave it as his*
> *opinion that landing in this great terrestrial crater would*
> *be extremely dangerous for an aviator because of the*
> *many treacherous air currents, and that the feat would*
> *probably not be attempted for some time to come.*

Many thought even if someone could land a plane in the canyon, it would be impossible to take off again, due to the short distance the pilot would have to get airborne and the overarching cliffs that would beckon a whirring propeller and the pilot behind it.

At the time, aviation was in its infancy. Although nineteen years out from the Wright brothers' historic flight at Kitty Hawk, North Carolina, few people had ever flown in a plane—and even fewer had ever piloted one. World War I trained many young men to fly combat planes, although America's one-year involvement in the "war to end all wars" was too brief to train a generation of fliers, as World War II later would. Flying was for the rich—or the crazy.

In 1922 Grand Canyon photographer Ellsworth Kolb felt the time was ripe to give a canyon landing a try. An aviation enthusiast (although not a pilot himself), Kolb didn't believe the common knowledge that a canyon landing was impossible. His opinion was undoubtedly influenced by his desire to record such a flight from the cockpit using a motion-picture camera, and to then show the film to amazed audiences willing to pay a healthy sum to see it.

Kolb soon found a pilot willing to attempt a canyon landing— Royal V. Thomas, a daredevil stunt pilot from Kansas, accustomed to death-defying flights to thrill audiences. The challenge intrigued Thomas, as likely did the publicity such a stunt would generate.

In early August 1922, Thomas flew his Lincoln Standard biplane to the airport at Williams, Arizona, 60 miles south of the national park. He hopped the train to the canyon to meet up with Kolb and look over potential landing sites. Riding mules into the canyon and along the Plateau Point Trail, they soon found a likely spot. With the permission of Grand Canyon National Park Superintendent Walter Crosby, Kolb, Thomas, and three park rangers cleared a 60- by 450-foot, nearly level runway on the Tonto Platform near Plateau Point. The landing strip had the added advantage of being in clear view from Grand Canyon Village, meaning the spectacular flight could be witnessed by a large crowd.

On August 8, Thomas fired up the engine of his biplane, Ellsworth filming from nearby as the plane prepared for take-off. They spent so much time getting establishing shots of the earthbound plane that they flooded the spark plugs with oil; the plugs had to be changed before they could finally get off the ground. At 9:10 A.M., Thomas and Ellsworth took to the skies, headed north toward the Grand Canyon.

At 9:50 A.M. the two men flew over the South Rim above the Bright Angel Hotel and Camp. Thomas circled the canyon to get a feel for the air currents, and then swooped low over the South Rim for Ellsworth to take pictures of El Tovar and other buildings in the village. Throngs of tourists waved and cheered with each pass the biplane made over the rim.

Then, it was time to get serious. A. Gaylord writes what happens next:

> *The motor was ticking as steadily as a clock. Up to the rim, and then, with a throttled motor, he dropped slowly over and down—down into the very bowels of the earth!*

> *The plane rocks a bit as it strikes an angry cross-current of air. Far, far below are rocks, rocks, rocks, and at the very bottom a silvery thread—the Colorado River. Bright Angel Trail creeps slowly up under the nose of the plane; then passes as slowly up and back behind, twisting and winding back and forth until lost from sight at the rim of this Devil's Bowl. Thomas looks over his shoulder and smiles.*

As they approached the landing strip, Thomas advised Kolb to loosen his seatbelt: The strip, which ended just shy of the edge of the cliff dropping some 1,200 feet to the river, didn't look long enough from the air. Thomas wanted to make sure both were unencumbered so they could leap from the plane rather than going over the cliff with it.

Thomas made one pass over the landing area and then climbed up and away, only to circle back, pull back on the throttle, wave to the crowd on the rim, and drop the biplane into a spinning freefall toward the landing site. A few hundred feet above the Tonto Platform, the aviator revved the engine and leveled the airplane. Thomas gently spiraled the plane down to the airstrip and touched down, bringing the biplane to a stop 50 feet shy of the edge of the Inner Gorge.

As the two men climbed from the biplane, wind whipped across the platform. Thomas and Kolb decided it would be best to wait a day for the winds to calm down before attempting to get the plane airborne and out of the canyon. The Fred Harvey Company supplied mules for the men to ascend the Bright Angel Trail to the South Rim. Once in the village, Thomas was informed that the wind had spun the biplane around, breaking off the tail skid and damaging a wing. The problems would need to be attended to the next morning.

After a good night's sleep on the South Rim, the two descended the Bright Angel. Upon arriving at the airplane, they set to work repairing the wind damage with baling wire and a spring from a broken-down car. Airworthy again, the two climbed into the two-seater and lined up the plane for takeoff.

At 10:12 A.M. on August 9, Thomas and Kolb took off, and the biplane soared above the Tonto Platform. Turning soon after they were airborne, the aviator circled the plane in a tight spiral, rapidly rising from the inner canyon. It took a mere five minutes to clear the rim, adding a second record to the adventure. Not only was Thomas the first person to land an airplane within the national park and within the Grand Canyon, he was also the first to take off from the inner canyon and bring an airplane down safely once over the rim.

A week and a half after the daring flight, the Fred Harvey Company paid Thomas to repeat the flight, this time with a Fox News Company photographer. The resulting film from this second trip, backed by the marketing and distribution muscle of Fox (and later the Santa Fe Railroad, which acquired the film from Fox), was shown across the country, while Ellsworth Kolb's film was largely forgotten.

THE KAIBAB DEER AFFAIR

- 1924 -

MOST OF US HAVE SEEN A SINGLE DEER OR a small herd of the quiet, skinny-legged animals bound away through trees when startled: At lightning speed they bounce back and forth herky-jerky, quickly finding the best escape route and disappearing from sight. In 1924 on the North Rim's Kaibab Plateau, panic gripped officials as the population of mule deer grew to a seemingly unsustainable level. Faced with several grim options, officials set their better judgment aside and supported a plan to herd and then drive—as in a cattle drive—5,000 to 10,000 mule deer from the Kaibab National Forest on the North Rim down into the Grand Canyon, across the Colorado River (the deer were expected to swim it), and up the narrow Tanner Trail to the South Rim. If it worked, officials believed, thousands of deer would avoid starvation. As an added bonus, there would also be more mule deer on the South Rim, to the delight of tourists.

But before we describe the events of December 1924, we need to back up a bit and look at how officials arrived at the conclusion that driving deer across the Grand Canyon was worth a try. In 1906 President Theodore Roosevelt set aside the Kaibab Plateau on the North Rim as the Grand Canyon National Game Preserve, providing protection for the game species on the land. As Roosevelt later wrote: "The national Government could do much by establishing its forest reserves as game reserves, and putting on a sufficient number of forest rangers who should be empowered to prevent all hunting on the reserves."

Despite such lofty words, in the first decade or so of the preserve, a single forest service employee, James T. "Uncle Jim" Owens, worked in Grand Canyon National Game Preserve—and he was a hunter. His exploits were funded by the government, including his salary and bounties paid for predators killed. Roosevelt himself went on a North Rim hunting trip with Owens, stalking mountain lions in the preserve in 1913. In a nutshell, it was seen as noble to hunt predators on the preserve, while hunting game species was outlawed. Owens later gave himself credit for shooting some 600 mountain lions on the plateau, an impossible-to-verify number that may have been grossly exaggerated. Regardless, the killing of predators—not only mountains lions, but coyotes and wolves as well—has often been blamed for the perceived irruption in the mule deer population of the Kaibab by the 1920s. But things may not have been that simple.

In the first decades of the twentieth century, at the same time Owens was killing predators in the preserve, livestock ranchers began to move out of the area, due to the cost of shipping cattle and sheep to market from the remote, railroad-less region, and to what was perceived as the declining condition of the range. Livestock competed with mule deer for browse. Fewer cattle on the range meant an increase in browsable vegetation, and the mule deer population slowly expanded due to the increased food supply.

Regardless of the reasons, by 1924 the U.S. Forest Service estimated the Kaibab deer herd at 26,000 head, perhaps five times the population when the preserve was created in 1906. Others put the herd total at 50,000 deer, an astonishing number unsupported by any scientific survey. Later researchers examining what happened on the Kaibab in 1924 postulated a frightful 100,000 deer may have browsed the forest. Although such pregnant estimates fueled the emotions that came to the fore in 1924, ultimately the exact number of deer mattered little. Officials by 1924 believed that the deer population on the plateau was unsustainable and that something had to be done immediately to avoid a catastrophic die-off.

In the summer of 1924, Secretary of Agriculture Henry C. Wallace appointed a "Kaibab Deer Investigating Committee," including four prominent leaders of groups ranging from the Boone and Crockett Club to the American Livestock Breeders Association to the National Parks Association. After surveying the conditions in Arizona, the committee recommended reducing the Kaibab deer herd by one-half. (The committee estimated the deer population at 25,000 deer, so their proposal called for the removal of 12,500 animals.) They suggested accomplishing this using three methods: (1) trapping deer and shipping them to good habitat that had few deer; (2) opening the area to licensed hunting; and/or (3) sending in government hunters to kill deer.

The committee's report did not sit well with the National Park Service, which prized the existence of abundant game on the Kaibab as an attraction for visitors to Grand Canyon National Park's North Rim, to the south of the game preserve. It was also widely believed that the deer were relatively tame, and therefore that hunting them was not "sporting"; it was seen as tantamount to shooting cattle. Regardless, the forest service allowed a limited hunt on the plateau in the fall of 1924. Hunters killed as many as 700 deer, much to the chagrin of the park service as well as the State of Arizona, which wanted to control hunting in the area despite the land's federal status. But in the eyes of the forest service, the hunt still left many thousands of excess deer on the plateau—with winter on the way.

Into this bureaucratic battle stepped George McCormick, a Flagstaff-based cattle rancher with a creative streak. McCormick suggested to the State of Arizona that he could organize a deer drive of thousands of head off the plateau, into the Grand Canyon, and up to the South Rim. Governor George W. P. Hunt fell behind the plan and lobbied the forest service to support the idea. The forest service, desperate for a solution to a problem that was becoming increasingly untenable, signed on.

At a price of $2.50 per animal, McCormick contracted to drive between 5,000 and 10,000 deer down off the North Rim onto the rugged Nankoweap Trail. They would descend some 6,000 feet to the river over 10 rocky miles. The hooved animals would swim the 300- to 400-foot width of the Colorado, then make their way up the narrow, unmaintained Tanner Trail to the South Rim, an elevation gain of about 5,000 feet over 8 miles. The treacherousness of the trails for animals is underscored by the experiences of George McCormick, who lost two horses on the Tanner Trail while making his way to the North Rim for the deer drive.

With such a loopy idea officially sanctioned by the state and federal government, the spectacle unfolding upon the Kaibab Plateau attracted enormous attention, including the interest of author Zane Grey, who would go on to write the novel *The Deer Stalker* (1925) based on what he witnessed, and moviemaker D. W. Griffith. Griffith brought a film crew to the preserve, with the goal of capturing the momentous undertaking on celluloid.

Seventy-two Navajos on foot and twenty-five white men on horseback, all hired by McCormick, gathered on the Kaibab in mid-December 1924. On December 16, the deer drive began. Mark Musgrave of the U.S. Biological Survey later filed a report describing what happened:

> *There was no organization whatsoever. Each man did as he thought best and the deer were simply scared from one place to another back and forth. . . . Three detachments of men were thrown out, two of Indians and one of white men. . . . At first it was a fairly straight line east and west as they were driving south. I tried to keep the deer throwed [sic] back in front of the drive on the east wing but found it impossible. Very soon I heard Indians hallooing and jingling bells in all directions, so I rode as fast as I could along the back of the line and found that it had taken the form of a[n upside-down] V with the point nearest the objective, which was the pass going into Saddle Canyon [the planned point of entry to the Grand Canyon]. The deer shed off on either side of the V and when the men arrived at the objective point there were no deer in front of the drive.*

Perhaps predictably, the mule deer did not herd together like cattle but bounced around every which way until they found an escape route. The men adjusted to the pinball action of the deer by collapsing their human corral, leaving the deer wide-open exits to the east and west. On top of that, a blizzard swirled around the operation that day, and the filmmakers captured none of the brouhaha.

So the mule deer of the Kaibab remained on the plateau, and, as it turned out, the greatly feared die-off over the winter of

1924–1925 never came to pass. Few deer actually starved to death that winter.

Interestingly, Zane Grey's fictional account of the deer drive and his advocacy of stopping predator control efforts by the government in order to return to a natural balance of the deer herd helped establish modern wildlife management principles. Although the killing of predators on the Kaibab may have only played a partial role in what people continued to believe had been a dramatic overpopulation of deer, the practice gained the most attention from the whole fiasco. Over time, bounties for killing predators were eliminated, and many years later the federal government implemented plans to reintroduce predators to historic ranges (though not yet on the Kaibab Plateau).

During a collective moment of insanity in 1924, a spotlight shined on the Kaibab Plateau. Although the Kaibab deer drive was a miserable failure that made the officials involved in the adventure look as crazy as the idea itself, the events there precipitated a long, national discussion about the relationships between predators and prey. It revealed the wisdom of nature over humans in managing its affairs.

BYPASSING BRIGHT ANGEL

- 1925 -

The South Kaibab Trail is one of the most spectacular trails in the United States. Most inner Grand Canyon rim-to-river trails follow a side canyon to the Colorado River—the footpath of least resistance. In addition, most trails in the canyon follow ancient Native American or wildlife routes. The South Kaibab, however, runs along a ridgeline over a large portion of its length, giving the hiker or mule rider the feeling of being on a mountaintop surrounded by the kaleidoscopic walls of the Grand Canyon. And it was built where no trail existed (except for a 2-mile section into the Inner Gorge). The underlying story of this remarkable trail reveals a decades-old, epic battle for control of routes to the inner canyon, a battle that didn't end until after the South Kaibab Trail's completion.

Beginning at the turn of the twentieth century, businessman Ralph Cameron managed to finagle control of the Bright Angel Trail, which runs from Grand Canyon Village to the Colorado River, by filing numerous mining claims along its route. The canyon was not yet a national park, and mining claims polka-dotted the landscape. In the case of Cameron, his interest lay less in the wealth he could extract from his mining claims and more in the wealth he could extract from tourists traveling to the bottom of the Grand Canyon.

Under the laws in effect at the time and later laws passed at the behest of the politically powerful Cameron, the "builder" of a trail was allowed to charge "tolls" to people using the trail. Cameron had financed the improvement of the Bright Angel Trail into a viable inner-canyon route as early as 1890, and he charged a $1.00 toll on all mule and horse riders descending the trail from 1903 until 1912. He retained limited control of the trail until a U.S. Supreme Court ruling in 1920 invalidated his mining claims along the trail. The Bright Angel Trail subsequently fell under the exclusive control of Coconino County (the Arizona county where the Grand Canyon is located). The National Park Service wouldn't gain control of the trail until 1928.

With such long-term political battles raging around the Bright Angel Trail, it is not surprising that, after 1919, the National Park Service sought to build their own trail to the river and wash their hands of the Bright Angel Trail problem. Over the next few years, the Fred Harvey Company, which built Phantom Ranch at the bottom of the canyon in 1922, also favored a new trail that would carry hikers and mule riders to their inner-canyon establishment. Soon after Grand Canyon National Park was founded on February 26, 1919, Acting Superintendent W. H. Peters initiated a survey for a new trail to the river. The trail would descend from the western side of Yaki Point, 4 miles east of Grand Canyon Village, to the bottom of the canyon.

After a county referendum authorizing the sale of the Bright Angel Trail to the National Park Service failed in the elections of November 4, 1924 (primarily due to a disinformation campaign by now U.S. Senator Ralph Cameron), an assertive National Park Service moved quickly to start construction on the South Kaibab. By November 20 Grand Canyon National Park officials had ordered construction supplies and contracted workers for the project. A budget of $50,000 was earmarked. Interestingly, much of the communication between Washington and the national park was sent in code, as Senator Cameron's brother-in-law, L. L. Ferrall, served as the postmaster of Grand Canyon.

The crews assembled at the South Rim on December 1. One crew of twenty men would start work from the bottom of the canyon, working its way up, while a second twenty-man crew would build the trail down from the rim. They would eventually meet somewhere in the middle. The lower crew began work on December 3, but a winter storm delayed any major work by the upper crew until December 11. The park service set the ambitious goal of May 1, 1925, for the completion of the 7.2-mile trail, which would plummet 4,500 feet along its length.

One of the issues that officials needed to resolve early on was deciding what to call the new trail. As the trail was conceived and construction began, it was referred to as the Yaqui, or Yaki, Trail, because it descended from a spot on the rim near Yaki Point. Fred Harvey Company officials lobbied for "Phantom Trail," arguing that the new trail led directly to the company's Phantom Ranch. An evocative name, certainly, but Fred Harvey officials were primarily interested in promoting Phantom Ranch. Grand Canyon Superintendent J. R. Eakin favored calling it the "Kaibab Trail," after the national forest and plateau on the North Rim. In December 1924 National Park Service Director Stephen T. Mather wrote Superintendent Eakin, noting the Fred Harvey Company's preferred name of "Phantom Trail," but adding decisively, "I think Kaibab is better, however, so let's do that." The Kaibab Trail it became, with the

"South" added after the reconstruction and renaming of the North Kaibab Trail from the river to the North Rim in 1928.

Bad weather in January, including heavy snow at high elevations near the rim, slowed down the upper crew significantly. The lower crew had more favorable conditions, including working roughly along the route of a crude pre-existing trail out of the Inner Gorge, and made faster progress.

Superintendent Eakin, in a report on trail progress to Washington officials in February 1925, noted the challenges of building a trail in the Grand Canyon: "The lower limestone strata," Eakin wrote, "known locally as the Blue Lime [Redwall Limestone], is giving us much more trouble than anticipated. As an index of hardness, at one place it required 17 freshly sharpened bits to drill a hole eight inches in depth." In the end, more than half of the South Kaibab Trail had to be blasted out of solid rock.

By this time it also became apparent that the trail was going to cost considerably more and take longer to construct than originally estimated. By the end of March, nearly the entire original budget for construction had been spent (some $48,000), primarily due to the unexpected difficulty in drilling through the rock. In addition to the damage to equipment caused by hard rock, large sections of sandstone sometimes collapsed under the stress of drilling and dynamiting. The bed of the trail had to be rebuilt in such instances, causing long delays in progress.

The South Kaibab Trail, however, was a priority, and additional money was appropriated and other funds were moved around in the park service's budget to accommodate the additional costs. Funds were reallocated from the national park's 1926 road budget, and $25,000 was pulled from the money budgeted to purchase the Bright Angel Trail, which needed a new home after the failure of the referendum the previous fall. When the money for the purchase of the

Bright Angel Trail was approved by the U.S. Congress, prescient legislators inserted language allowing for such a transfer if the negotiations over acquisition of the Bright Angel failed. Although some emphatic letters requesting immediate infusions of cash were sent from Grand Canyon officials to National Park Service Director Mather in February and March 1925, the project had sufficient financial backing to guarantee the trail would be completed. The urgency of the letters reflected the still-poisonous political climate in northern Arizona, where many entities who had opposed the sale of the Bright Angel longed for the failure of the new trail construction project.

The two work crews finally met up in mid-June 1925, about six weeks behind the original, ambitious schedule. On June 15, 1925, Congressmen Louis Crampton and Carl Hayden (Hayden would defeat Ralph Cameron in 1926, taking over the polarizing senator's seat) dedicated the South Kaibab Trail. New Grand Canyon Superintendent M. R. Tillotson, declared the South Kaibab a "first class trail . . . easily the best trail in any national park."

In 1926 Fred Harvey mule corrals and stables, as well as a bunkhouse for mule packers, were built near the trailhead, with similar park service facilities added in 1929. The Kaibab Suspension Bridge across the Colorado River, a swaying, rickety affair built in 1921, was replaced by a sturdier, steel bridge in 1928, allowing easier and safer access to Phantom Ranch for South Kaibab mule riders and hikers.

Today, the South Kaibab Trail is a principal South-Rim-to-river route at Grand Canyon, and the trail favored by cross-canyon hikers bound for the North Rim. Built to end a divisive political battle, the sky-high trail, with its pitched descent to the Colorado River, remains one of the most spectacular trails in the country.

THE HONEYMOONERS

- 1928 -

AH, TO HONEYMOON AT THE GRAND CANYON. Better yet, thought newlyweds Glen and Bessie Hyde in the summer of 1928, to honeymoon *through* the Grand Canyon. Glen was an experienced sweep-scow boatman, deeply familiar with the piloting of the favored boats of Salmon River runners in his native Idaho. His petite bride Bessie enthusiastically agreed to the daring honeymoon plans.

Just two years earlier, the possibility of such a honeymoon was probably the last thing on Bessie Haley's mind. On June 5, 1926, Bessie married a different man, high school friend Earl Helmick. But by the end of the summer, she was studying art in San Francisco at the California School of Fine Arts, and she was alone.

Why Bessie and Earl parted company is not known, but there is circumstantial evidence suggesting Bessie was pregnant—perhaps the reason for the marriage in the first place—and she may have had an abortion or miscarriage in California, or possibly put her child up for adoption. Pregnant or not, Bessie continued her art studies until late February 1927.

While in San Francisco, Bessie struck up a friendship with Eraine Granstedt, a nude model at the art school with aspirations of Hollywood stardom. For some of her stay in California, Bessie lived with Eraine and her brother Theodore at their place, ironically, on San Francisco's Hyde Street.

But by late February, both Bessie and Eraine were ready for something new. They bought passage on a ship to Los Angeles, packed up their meager belongings, and set sail. As it turned out, that southbound cruise changed both of their lives dramatically. Eraine changed her name to Greta, billing herself to Hollywood casting agents as a Swedish starlet. It worked in a way, as Granstedt won small roles in B-movies for many years. Meanwhile, on the ship, Bessie met a handsome, athletic Idahoan named Glen Hyde.

Glen and Bessie were smitten with each other, and by November 1927, Bessie moved to Elko, Nevada, a couple of hours south of the Idaho border, with the goal of establishing residency in a state with relatively nonrestrictive divorce laws so she could end her marriage to Earl Helmick and marry Glen. On February 21, 1928, she filed for divorce on the grounds of "non-support." Helmick did not respond to the resulting papers that soon showed up at his door in Ohio, and on April 11, a Nevada judge granted Bessie her divorce. The next morning, she married Glen Hyde in Twin Falls, Idaho, and they settled into married life at Glen's farm near Murtaugh, about 30 miles southeast of Twin Falls. They would take their honeymoon after the fall harvest.

In October 1928, the newlyweds made their way to Green River, Utah, where Glen set to work building himself a sweep scow 20 feet long, 5 feet wide, and 3 feet deep. The boat looked something like flat-bottomed swamp boats that were poled through the bayous of the American South, with the addition of long, hockey-stick–like oars stretching out from the bow and the stern; the oars, or sweeps, were to be operated by a person precariously balanced on a platform near the center of the boat. Green Riverites found the boat curious, and some came down to the river to watch Glen hammer away. One, Harry Howland, thought the boat looked "like a floating coffin." Another, Bill Reeder, questioned Glen about their plan, and later regarded the boatbuilder as "surly, conceited and stoopid."

Regardless of the opinions of locals, the Hydes pushed off in their newly constructed sweep scow on October 20, 1928. They planned to reach Needles, California, on December 9, where Glen's father, R. C. Hyde, would be waiting for them.

They carried plenty of gear and provisions in their large boat, including crates of canned produce, potatoes, a hunting rifle, and a barrel full of sand and ash that would be doused in kerosene and set afire for boat-board cooking. Perhaps the Hydes felt the ground would be too hard for sleeping in the canyons of the Southwest: They counted a set of bedsprings and a mattress among necessities brought on the trip.

Over the years, there has been much talk about one thing the Hydes did not carry onboard: life jackets. By 1928 life jackets were common among Colorado River runners. But before we wag our twenty-first-century fingers at Glen and Bessie for this omission, we have to look at their trip in context. Glen was not a Colorado River runner when they set off on their honeymoon; he was an Idaho sweep-scow boatman. Among his kind, life jackets were unheard of. As with their goofy boat, the Hydes brought with them ideas that were quite common in the Pacific Northwest.

The Hydes headed south on the Green River through the relatively calm water between Green River (the town) and the confluence of the Green and Colorado. Shortly thereafter, they entered Cataract Canyon, 40 river miles of nasty whitewater. They made it through, somehow, and floated on through placid Glen Canyon, reaching Lees Ferry on November 7, 1928.

Today, Lees Ferry marks the northern boundary of Grand Canyon National Park. The Hydes spent the night, chatting it up with river runners and ferrymen who lingered around the site despite the closure of the namesake ferry earlier that year. By the next afternoon, they had forged ahead into Marble Canyon.

Mile after mile and rapid after rapid, the Hydes floated on. They reached the then-boundary of Grand Canyon National Park on November 11 and soon were thoroughly abused by the river in Sockdolager Rapid. Glen was smacked on the chin by the end of the sweep while negotiating the rapid, the impact knocking him overboard. Bessie helped haul her soggy husband back into the boat.

The next day, they reached the foot of the newly constructed South Kaibab Trail, and they hiked out the 7 miles to the South Rim, intent on re-supplying and getting a good night's sleep. Bessie was suitably impressed by the views from perhaps the most spectacular of inner-canyon trails, writing: "You could see for miles—wonderful cliffs that changed all the time as the light changed."

While in Grand Canyon Village, they met up with Emery Kolb, the pioneering Grand Canyon photographer who had been down the river through the entire canyon twice. Kolb offered life jackets and suggested they acquire at least some inner tubes, but the Idahoans declined. They spent one more night in the comfort of the village before setting down the Bright Angel Trail the next morning to resume their trip.

At the river, they found Adolph Sutro, a wealthy California tourist, looking over their boat. After some discussions about what the Hydes were doing and how they operated their odd boat, Sutro convinced them to take him along for the ride to Hermit Creek, a few miles downstream and the site of the next trail out to the rim. The Hydes agreed, and Sutro joined them for a short sweep-scow jaunt.

Writer Brad Dimock, who exhaustively investigated the Hydes' trip and disappearance in his remarkable book *Sunk without a Sound* (2001), related that Sutro was impressed with neither the Hydes' boat nor Glen's river-running skills. Sutro took the last photograph taken of the couple. The photograph has fueled much speculation, as both looked quite tense—almost angry. The grim couple may have had grave doubts about completing the trip. Some have speculated that the photograph shows tension between the two that may be pre-cursory to whatever trouble they ran into farther downriver. Or maybe Sutro just bugged them, and they wanted him to take the damn picture already.

They pushed off from the riverbank at Hermit Creek on November 18, 1928. The Hydes were never seen again.

As December 9 came and went, R. C. Hyde waited for his son and his new bride in Needles, 375 miles downriver from Hermit Creek. He didn't wait long, as he quickly recognized something was terribly wrong. He traveled to Las Vegas and immediately began pres-suring the powers that be to launch a full-scale search-and-rescue operation. Through the governors of Idaho and West Virginia, the lat-ter where Bessie Hyde's parents lived, the request for help reached the offices of President Calvin Coolidge and his Secretary of War, Dwight Davis. On December 17, Davis ordered an air search of the Colorado River corridor in Grand Canyon for the missing honeymooners.

The two airplanes sent by the federal government, flying unnerv-ingly low above the Colorado, through the towering cliffs of the Inner Gorge, spotted the Hydes' sweep scow on December 19, float-ing undisturbed near River Mile 237, 142 miles downstream from Hermit Creek. There was no sign of the couple, but a still-afloat boat was undoubtedly a good sign.

Aware of the discovery of the sweep scow, a search party consist-ing of Emery Kolb, his brother Ellsworth Kolb, R. C. Hyde, and

Grand Canyon National Park Chief Ranger Jimmy Brooks made their way to the mouth of Diamond Creek, the site of an old dam-site-surveying camp and one of the few places below Hermit Creek with access to the Colorado River in the Grand Canyon. On December 22 the search team began patching an old boat at the survey site, and they launched their search on Christmas Eve. The Kolbs and Brooks made the journey, as the boat was not big enough for all four.

They reached the sweep scow on Christmas Day, having found no trace of the Hydes upriver. The scow, too, revealed no sign of the couple. It floated in calm water, held in place by a bowline attached to something underwater. The search team found the Hydes' gear intact in the boat, including Bessie's camera and film, her diary, Glen's gun, and their warm clothes. The last entry in the diary was November 30. The searchers removed the most important items and then cut the scow loose, an action that led to later speculation that the body of one of the Hydes may have been wrapped around the other end of the bowline, snagged in boulders or other debris on the river bottom. They continued downriver, where they then hiked out to Peach Springs to meet up with R. C. Hyde on December 27.

Searches continued into January, spurred by R. C. Hyde's conviction that the couple may have left the river upstream from Diamond Creek. But the outside world lost hope that the pair would ever be found, and Hyde soon found himself wandering the plateaus and canyons of the lower part of the Grand Canyon all alone. He found nothing.

Much later, in the 1970s, a story grew among river runners that a woman claiming to be Bessie Hyde, one Liz Cutler of Ohio, had gone down the river on a commercial run with Grand Canyon Expeditions. Despite later hype, including a 1987 pseudo-documentary about the Hydes and Cutler on the TV show *Unsolved Mysteries*, writer Dimock clearly demonstrates in his book that it was nearly impossible for Liz Cutler and Bessie Hyde to have been the same person. Similarly, the odd discovery of Glen and Bessie Hyde's marriage certificate among the possessions of Georgie Clark, a long-time river runner in Grand Canyon, after Clark's death in 1992, led to rumors that Clark and Bessie were one and the same. Dimock also examines the evidence of this and concludes convincingly that this was not possible. A simple comparison of photographs of the two leads one to wholly agree with Dimock. The reason Clark had the marriage certificate, however, has never been explained.

The Colorado River in the Grand Canyon is a mighty stream that still thrills and terrifies river runners today. As historians have noted, the Colorado of the past rarely turned up its dead; most who drowned on the river have never been recovered. The case of the Hydes is strange indeed, but the fact that no trace of them has ever been found is more the rule than the exception.

HAZARDOUS DUTY

- 1933–1936 -

THE COLORADO RIVER SHIMMIES THROUGH THE INNER GORGE of the
Grand Canyon nearly a mile below Grand Canyon Village on the
South Rim. In 1933 hikers and mule riders could get to Phantom
Ranch, just up Bright Angel Creek from the Colorado, via the South
Kaibab Trail and the Kaibab Suspension Bridge, a distance of approximately 7 miles from the trailhead. But the South Kaibab Trail left
the rim several miles east of the village, and the main route to the
river directly from the village, the Bright Angel Trail, was not connected in the Inner Gorge to the river crossing. Those hiking in from
the village veered east just below Indian Garden and followed the
Tonto Trail on the Tonto Platform, eventually accessing the South
Kaibab Trail. It was a laborious, detour-filled slog of nearly 12 miles
to Phantom Ranch along this route.

In 1929 Grand Canyon National Park Superintendent M. R.
Tillotson, an engineer by training, worked with a small group of officials to draw up initial plans for building a trail into the cliff wall of

the Vishnu basement rocks of the Inner Gorge, from the terminus of the Bright Angel Trail at Pipe Creek on the Colorado River to the South Kaibab Trail above the bridge—a distance of roughly 2 miles. Such a trail would shorten the hike from Grand Canyon Village to Phantom Ranch via the Bright Angel Trail by at least 3 hot, dusty miles. But lacking money and manpower, the ambitious trail, which would be far more challenging to build than any other route in the Grand Canyon, remained on the drawing board.

Later that year, however, Black Tuesday changed everything. On October 29, 1929, the stock market collapsed. In the aftermath, banks closed, unemployment soared, and vast stretches of the fertile Great Plains dried up under a cruelly coincidental drought. The country lurched forward into the Great Depression.

One of the jobs lost during the Great Depression was that of the president of the United States, Herbert Hoover, who lost the 1932 election to the governor of New York, Franklin D. Roosevelt. President Roosevelt took office on March 4, 1933, and he immediately initiated bills and policies that he hoped would provide relief to the weary country. On March 21 the new president called on Congress to establish a federal organization to employ young men in conservation activities on public land. Congress passed the bill ten days later, and on April 5, when President Roosevelt appointed Robert Fechner director of the Emergency Conservation Works, the agency that would coordinate the conservation efforts, the Civilian Conservation Corps (CCC) was born.

It didn't take long for the CCC to reach Grand Canyon National Park. In May 1933 Company 818 of the CCC formed at Arizona's Fort Huachuca, and moved to Grand Canyon that summer.

Company 818 of the CCC went to work immediately, fighting fires in the Kaibab National Forest, transporting equipment and supplies too heavy for mules to the Bright Angel Camp (including a tram cable and a pool table), rebuilding the transcanyon telephone line, maintaining the North and South Kaibab Trails, performing road construction on the rims, building low stone walls along the Rim Trail in Grand Canyon Village, and constructing picnic areas and other recreational facilities for tourists.

With the arrival of the CCC workers, Superintendent Tillotson revived the plan for a trail along the Colorado River in the Inner Gorge. The CCC agreed to take on the trail's construction, and work began on November 1, 1933.

Along the 2-mile proposed route of the trail on the southern side of the Colorado River, the sheer cliff of schist and granite soars 1,700 feet above the water. The 2-mile trail would be cut into the cliff face, undulating along a route between 50 and 400 feet above the Colorado.

The Colorado River Trail (often shortened to the "River Trail" today) got its name by default. It was decided to name the new trail after the first worker killed during the trail's construction; remarkably, no man lost his life during the perilous work, and the name remained.

In addition to the difficulty of building a trail along a sheer cliff, the work site had the added disadvantage of having no roads anywhere nearby. All equipment came down the trail from the rim, usually on the backs of mules, but loads more than 200 pounds were too much for the mules. With strong men in abundance, the CCC put them to work moving the heavy stuff. Louis Purvis, a supervisor of the trail's construction and later the author of *The Ace in the Hole: A Brief History of Company 818 of the Civilian Conservation Corps,* wrote that one such project involved moving two compressors (for jackhammers) from the South Kaibab trailhead to the river. Twenty men climbed out the South Kaibab Trail to the South Rim to fetch the machines, and they loaded each one on a sled designed specifically to carry the compressors down the trail. Two hardwood poles attached to the contraptions were used to steer each sled around the South Kaibab's legendary switchbacks, while a rope in front was used to pull a sled, and a rope in back was used to slow a sled down when it got moving too fast. With each compressor, two enrollees manned the poles, while five pulled the compressor forward and three kept it from becoming a runaway. Slowly, meticulously, the heavy loads descended into the canyon; on a descent that takes a lightly loaded hiker perhaps two to three hours to complete, the workers needed two *days* to deliver the compressors.

The hazards of the work site were many, but landslides were arguably the most feared. The cliff didn't always come down when and where the workers wanted. Purvis relates a story in his book that could have given the Colorado River Trail a very long and complicated name if it hadn't been for the shrewd observation skills of Supervisor A. T. Sevey. One warm day in 1934, while watching his men and the cliff face from a short distance away, Sevey slowly rose and ordered the crew leader, in a calm voice, to have the workers pull back to where he was sitting with their equipment. When the men gathered around, Sevey smiled and said, "Sit down boys and rest a few minutes." Less than ten minutes later, seemingly without warning, the cliff face gave way, crushing the section of trail where the men had been working. Sevey then turned to the crew and said, "Okay, boys, you may go back to work now."

In the fall of 1934, another section of the cliff face gave way, carrying two workers over the edge on a bouncy drop of some 150 feet to the river. Miraculously, the men survived, although their injuries were quite serious. After evacuation from the accident site, the men were treated in the camp hospital. One eventually rejoined his crew, while the other asked for a discharge from the CCC and returned home.

Work progressed steadily—although slowly—and on January 20, 1936, the first pack mule train used the Colorado River Trail to access Phantom Ranch. The trip from the village to Phantom Ranch had been shortened to a little over 9 miles, a more reasonable distance, at least for the hearty.

The CCC remained in operation until 1942, and many of its well-trained men became the backbone of the U.S. Army in World War II. The CCC's legacy at Grand Canyon can be seen throughout the park in many of the trails, decorative and protective walls, picnic ramadas, and roads. The River Trail is still in use today as the main route for mule trains traveling to Phantom Ranch and for hikers wishing to access the South Kaibab Trail from the Bright Angel. There is a tendency to assume when hiking in the inner canyon that the trails have always been there, but the work of the CCC and of modern-day National Park Service trail crews make inner-canyon travel possible. Without the dangerous efforts of these workers, hiking in the Grand Canyon would be a far more perilous adventure than it is today.

SOMEWHERE IN THE GRAND CANYON

- 1944 -

P ARACHUTING INTO THE G RAND C ANYON IN BROAD DAYLIGHT would be a bad idea. At 2:00 A.M. on June 21, 1944, three Army Air Corps fliers tumbled out of a B-24 bomber over the Grand Canyon *in darkness* while en route from an airbase near Tonopah, Nevada, to Tucson, after the airplane developed engine trouble. The pilot and copilot ordered Lieutenant Charles Goldblum, Flight Officer Maurice Cruickshank Jr., and Corporal Roy Embanks to bail out when the plane lost some 15,000 feet in altitude as the engine sputtered. Unaware of their location, the three fliers leapt into darkness and floated toward the earth below.

Strong winds pulled at the parachutists, but none could recognize that they were now descending into the Grand Canyon. Flight Officer Cruickshank and Corporal Embanks landed on the broad Tonto Platform on the north side of the Colorado River, but Lieutenant Goldblum landed just over the lip of the platform, snagging his parachute on rocks. Although he now dangled 1,200 feet above the Colorado River, the airman remained unaware that he was in the Grand Canyon; sensing danger, however, he decided to remain still until daylight, when he could assess his predicament.

After dropping another 2,000 feet, the B-24 sputtered back to life, and the pilot and co-pilot landed the plane safely at the Kingman Army Airfield, 100 miles southwest of where the three men had bailed out of the plane. They alerted authorities at the base, who then contacted the Coconino County Sheriff's Department. On the morning of June 22, Sheriff Peery Francis drove from Flagstaff to the South Rim in search of the missing fliers. Deputy Sheriff Charley Halliday searched the desert near Cameron, 60 miles east of Grand Canyon Village. Neither man could locate the fliers, and they soon came to the conclusion that they were probably somewhere in the canyon.

As dawn came on June 22, Lieutenant Goldblum took in the scale of his situation. Acting quickly, he braced himself on a narrow ledge and then slowly pulled himself up the shroud lines of his snagged parachute. The parachute held, and he was able to pull himself up and over the edge of the Inner Gorge to the relative safety of the Tonto Platform. A short while later, he found Flight Officer Cruickshank, who had broken a bone in his foot when he hit the ground.

Looking in one direction, the two airmen could see they were on a broad shelf studded with blackbrush and prickly pear cacti. To the north, high cliffs blocked escape; to the south, a dark gorge stretched through the plateau as far as they could see to the east and west. As the sun lit up pastel shades of the inner-canyon rock layers, Goldblum and Cruickshank correctly guessed they must have landed in the Grand Canyon. If either were British, they would have described this situation as a "sticky wicket."

A short distance away, Corporal Embanks was also taking in his predicament. Alone on the Tonto Platform, he spread out his parachute on the ground in an attempt to signal search planes of his location. Two days later, Goldblum and Cruickshank spotted Embanks's parachute, and they made their way across the Tonto Platform to the third flier. Cruickshank was able to move slowly using a tree branch as a makeshift crutch. The two fliers spread out their parachutes next to Embanks's, and the three waited for help.

Temperatures climb over 100° Fahrenheit on the Tonto Platform during the summer, and water sources are few and far between. Shade is rare. Searching for a route out of the canyon, Goldblum found a small spring; he and Corporal Embanks were able to bring water back to Cruickshank in their boots.

Meanwhile, the search for the missing fliers continued from Grand Canyon Village, the North Rim, and Kingman Army Airfield. On June 26, five days after the airmen had bailed out of their plane, search planes from Kingman spotted the parachutes. A short time later, they dropped K-rations, water, and a walkie-talkie to the men.

The men were on the north side of the Colorado River, about 18 miles northwest of Grand Canyon Village. They were on the Tonto Platform some 5,000 feet below the North Rim's remote Point Sublime. After conferring with National Park Service rangers, it became clear to Army officials that the men were in a nearly inaccessible area of the Grand Canyon.

Although helicopter technology was advancing by 1944, there were no working models believed capable of landing on the Tonto Platform in the canyon. It was widely believed that flying a helicopter into the canyon would lead inevitably to the crash of such a craft due to the air currents in the gorge, and the idea of a helicopter rescue of the men was not considered.

A ground party headed into the canyon from the South Rim, hauling a dismantled river boat on the backs of mules and hoping to reach the south bank of the river where, again hoping, they could cross the Colorado. The three fliers could then climb down to them.

A second ground party descended with a harpoon gun they planned to use to shoot a line across the river. Both parties eventually turned back, the first because the flood-swollen Colorado precluded a crossing and the latter because they were unable to secure the harpoon in the hard rock on the other side of the gorge. Meanwhile, airplanes dropped more supplies to the men, including additional K-rations and water, medical supplies, cigarettes, blankets, and a note informing the men that they were in the Grand Canyon and to stay near the parachutes.

During the rescue attempts, inner-canyon mule trips for tourists were suspended, as the mules and all backcountry rangers were pulled from duty in case they were needed to assist with the rescue.

From the air, Colonel Donald Phillips, commander of the Kingman Army Airfield, surveyed and took photographs along the North Rim, as well as in the canyon near the fliers. Returning to the base, he examined the photographs and determined there was a possible route, unknown to the park service, down to the Tonto Platform from the North Rim. The only way to find out if it was a viable route was to send a team to attempt a descent.

Meanwhile, Dr. Alan A. MacRae, an Old Testament scholar from a seminary in Delaware, was heading down the North Kaibab Trail with his new bride, on an inner-canyon hike to Clear Creek. Dr. MacRae was enjoying his fourteenth trip into the Grand Canyon, and the hiker was widely considered one of the most experienced Grand Canyon backcountry hikers of his day. A hiker using an emergency phone near Ribbon Falls was asked if he could contact Dr. MacRae. The professor and his bride happened to be hiking nearby, and they received the message to return to the North Rim to aid in a rescue attempt from that side of the canyon.

The rescue team consisted of Dr. MacRae and veteran park service ranger Ed Laws. Colonel Phillips had spotted a talus break in the

Redwall below Grama Point, 6 miles east of Point Sublime. Dr. MacRae and Laws studied the Army aerial photographs, and agreed with the colonel that a descent from Grama might be possible. As far as the men could tell from the photographs, it appeared to be the only possible route from the North Rim down to the Tonto Platform and the three fliers.

The men began their descent on June 28, and after spending the night at a spring, they descended into the Tuna Creek drainage and reached the three fliers around 10:00 A.M. on June 29, a little more than eight days after the trio's stay in the Grand Canyon had begun. The rescuers had discovered a previously unknown route in reaching the airmen.

Aiding Flight Officer Cruickshank, the five men worked their way back up the route. They camped the night of June 29 at the spring Dr. MacRae and Laws had discovered, and they reached the North Rim at 12:45 P.M. on June 30. The men were badly sunburned and Cruickshank's toe needed to be set, but otherwise they were healthy and in good spirits.

"We lived in comparative luxury after we got together and the planes dropped us supplies," Corporal Embanks told reporters.

The men were fed and then began a 225-mile trip to the canyon's South Rim by truck. From there they drove on to the Kingman Army Airfield, and their unplanned Grand Canyon adventure came to an end.

GRAND CANYON ENTERS
THE ATOMIC AGE

- 1951 -

The residents of Hiroshima, Japan, saw or felt the flash of the explosion before they heard the roar of the detonation. Some experienced neither; at the precise moment of the blast, thousands simply ceased to exist. On August 6, 1945, at 8:15 A.M., the United States dropped an atomic bomb on the Japanese city. Three days later, the United States dropped a second bomb on the Japanese city of Nagasaki. By the middle of August, the Japanese surrendered, and World War II, a conflict that had resulted in the deaths of some forty million people, finally ended. But the military writer Bernard Brodie recognized that the detonation of the two atomic bombs had changed everything. "Everything about the atomic bomb," he wrote, "is overshadowed by the twin facts that it exists and its destructive power is fantastically great."

After the Soviet Union detonated its own atomic bomb a little more than four years later, a shocked United States stepped up both nuclear research and the search for uranium to fuel America's arsenal. The Cold War and its symptom, the nuclear arms race, had begun. Mining uranium became a matter of national security, trumping all other concerns. As the politicians and generals saw it, America's survival was at stake.

In 1893, some fifty-two years before the detonation of the Hiroshima bomb, prospector Dan Hogan discovered a promising copper outcropping on the wall of the Grand Canyon, more than 1,000 feet below the rim. The canyon was not yet a national park, and mining activity existed on claims all over the region. In 1906 Hogan and his partner Charles Babbitt patented the copper claim, with four acres on the South Rim along today's Hermit Road just east of Powell Point, and sixteen acres cascading down the canyon wall. Hogan, who acquired sole control of the mine in 1912, mined only modest amounts of copper over the years at his small operation, known as the Orphan Lode claim, but he did retain title to the claim. In 1936, with Grand Canyon now a national park, Hogan opened the Grand Canyon Trading Post (later renamed the Grand Canyon Inn) at the site, hoping to cash in on the increasing number of tourists visiting the canyon.

In 1951 some amateur prospectors snooping around the site discovered radioactive materials at the Orphan Lode claim. Atomic Energy Commission (AEC) geologists confirmed the discovery: The Orphan Lode claim contained high-grade uranium. Within four years, after further tests by Western Gold and Uranium, which now owned the property, the first shipment of uranium left the South Rim. Trucked to an AEC ore-buying station at Tuba City, east of the Grand Canyon on the Navajo Reservation, the ore proved to be some of the highest-grade uranium ever mined in the United States. Although an operational mine on the rim of the Grand Canyon seems strange today, removing the ore was legal. The land was a privately controlled mining camp that happened to be surrounded by a national park.

Western Gold built a tramway 1,800 feet down the side of the Grand Canyon at the site. The tram could carry forty-five tons of ore daily, lifting it from the mine opening on the canyon wall to the rim. After the construction of a Tuba City uranium mill, which could profitably process lower-grade ore, the mining company invested heavily in what was now known as the Orphan Mine. They drilled a 1,600-foot elevator shaft to the mine, which not only carried out the ore but also ferried workers to and from the site. The elevator dropped at a stomach-churning 820 feet per minute. A 1,200-foot horizontal shaft extended from the elevator to the mine workings. The underground facilities included a machine shop and lunchroom, and dormitories for miners hugged the canyon wall on the talus slope of the Hermit Formation. Western Gold also built infrastructure on the rim, including a water tank, bunkhouses, offices, and a mess hall. They even catered to tourists, selling uranium samples at the Grand Canyon Inn, which continued to operate on the site while the miners worked below.

Although the National Park Service was not pleased about the mining operation, the two entities peacefully coexisted—initially. The park service even granted permission for Western Gold to build an access road on park land to a railroad siding, allowing the company to ship ore more cheaply via the rail lines of the Grand Canyon Railway. But in 1960, Western Gold ignited a battle that brought nationwide attention to the little mine in a national park, and the days of peaceful coexistence ended.

Under a complex provision of mining law, Western Gold claimed it had the right to mine uranium under parkland, as long as the uranium was connected to the initial lode under the twenty-acre claim. The Department of the Interior, which oversees the National Park Service, disagreed, asserting the mining company had no right to uranium under the national park. The lines were drawn in the sandstone.

Rather than take the government to court, the chairman of Western Gold, Richard Ince, launched a public-relations offensive that was so successful, he soon found his company allied with environmentalists and Arizona's congressional delegation. In the summer of 1961, Ince announced to the world that the company was considering building a 400-room hotel *down the wall of the Grand Canyon* on the site. The wily chairman suggested that the hotel was a back-up plan Western Gold would pursue if they were not allowed to mine uranium under the national park.

Newspapers throughout the country picked up the story, almost all taking the view that the hotel was a monstrosity that would ruin one of America's greatest scenic treasures. This is exactly what Western Gold wanted; those against the hotel were by default for the mining of uranium under the national park. All over the country, concerned citizens wrote letters to their representatives and to newspapers criticizing the hotel plan. Congress responded by passing legislation in 1962 that would allow the company to mine uranium under parkland for twenty-five years in return for agreeing to turn over title to the original Orphan Lode claim to the government within six months of passage of the bill, and to close the Grand Canyon Inn by 1966. The legislation passed, and President John F. Kennedy signed it into law. With the stroke of a pen, a national park would be mined.

Throughout the 1960s, Western Gold (which was acquired by several companies and changed names multiple times) mined uranium under the original claim and beneath adjoining parkland. The right to pursue uranium under the park proved to be hugely profitable for the company, as some 60 percent of the uranium taken from the Orphan Mine over the years came from lodes underneath the park.

But the days of milk and honey were to be short lived. In 1966 the Tuba City processing mill closed, and the next year, the Orphan

Mine was acquired by the Cotter Corporation, which processed uranium for private energy companies. However, the company's mill was in Colorado, and the cost to transport the ore from the Grand Canyon to that mill was too high to be profitable. On April 25, 1969, the Orphan Mine closed for good.

Although the National Park Service owned the land, Cotter's lease to mine the site lasted until 1987. The company negotiated with the park service to sell the mining rights to the government, and, in the 1970s, considered reopening the mine, but ultimately the site remained unused until the lease ran out.

Today, the mine remains sealed with the surrounding land on the rim fenced off to protect visitors. Low-level radiation exists in the area, and the park service strongly warns visitors of the dangers at the site. The Rim Trail, which once followed the edge of the canyon past the mine, detours around the site. Inner-canyon hikers on the Tonto Trail are warned not to drink water from the intermittent flow of Horn Creek, which has its source directly below the Orphan Mine. The park service has erected an interpretive sign at Powell Point, from which visitors can view the mine's headframe near the canyon's edge.

DIPS IN THE COLORADO

- 1955 -

WHAT IS IT ABOUT THE GRAND CANYON THAT CAUSES PEOPLE to leave
common sense at the rims or on the riverbank at Lees Ferry? According
to Thomas M. Myers and Michael P. Ghiglieri in their eye-opening
book *Over the Edge: Death in Grand Canyon,* more than 700 people
have suffered traumatic deaths at the canyon over the years. Some
deaths are accidents, of course, such as the bad luck of being in the
path of a landslide (or of a single rock thrown from the rim), or
attempting to move in for a photograph with one eye looking
through the viewfinder—and stepping off the rim. Still others make
one or a series of poor choices, such as hiking in the canyon without
sufficient water and food, trying to hike too far for conditions in the
canyon, or stepping out too close to the rim to "see what's down
there." And then there is the occasional publicity-seeking stunt. In
1955 Southern Californians Bill Beer and John Daggett attempted
something that fit these last two categories; despite their determina-
tion to make decision after poor decision in pursuit of their fifteen

minutes of fame, the two bucked the odds—they lived. On Easter Sunday 1955, Beer and Daggett jumped into the Colorado River at Lees Ferry and began their attempt to swim through the Grand Canyon.

The Colorado River winds 277 river miles through the canyon. In 1955 the river was not yet regulated by Glen Canyon Dam. The temperature of the water fluctuated with the seasons, and the two swimmers dipped into water considerably warmer than today. Currently, the flow in the Colorado River squeezes through conduits deep below the surface of Lake Powell at Glen Canyon Dam, and the released water stays consistently in the forties through the upper half of the canyon.

The funny thing about this whole endeavor is that Beer and Daggett were successful: They became the first people to swim through the Grand Canyon. At the time of their swim, only a few hundred people had ever been through the canyon *in boats,* as commercial river rafting didn't take off until the 1960s, when Glen Canyon Dam predictably regulated the river's flow.

Beer and Daggett did research, reading many books on the Colorado River and the Grand Canyon, but they routinely discounted views that the river or the canyon was dangerous. On a limited budget, they purchased cheap rubber suits and long johns, and rubber boxes designed for World War II radio gear to hold their equipment and food. Some movie-making friends convinced them they might be able to make some money selling footage of their adventure, so they splurged on a 16mm movie camera and lots of film. As Beer noted in his book about the trip, *We Swam the Grand Canyon* (1988), the camera and film "really blew our budget to smithereens. We coulda bought a boat."

Before their departure, the swimmers took time for interviews with the *Los Angeles Times* and a local TV station, although they made the reporters agree not to publish or broadcast the material until they were afloat in the Colorado. The seriousness of the interviews, in which the reporters seemed to be gathering material for the men's obituaries, helped Beer and Daggett realize that their "cheap, private little lark" had gotten a little out of hand. Oddly, though, this realization led primarily to introspection on whether they would be taken seriously, whether they would make any money on their film, and whether the trip would change their lives. Although they each prepared a will before they left Los Angeles, the two did not spend a lot of time ruminating on the truly horrific danger they were about to expose themselves to.

When the pair first waded into the river at Lees Ferry, the water felt "pleasant." But before they reached Navajo Bridge, a few miles downstream, "the cold water began to get downright uncomfortable," Beer wrote. As it turned out, their rubber suits leaked. When they got to camp, they found out their rubberized boxes did, too. They had double-wrapped some of their clothes in plastic bags, but some clothes, as well as the movie camera, were soaked. After that first day, at least for Beer, it finally set in that what they were doing was exceedingly dangerous. "Dropping off to sleep," Beer wrote, "I wondered what the rapids would be like. Would we be able to get through? Or would we be hurt—a leg broken, or a concussion? And what if we got pinned to a rock by the current?"

They would soon find out the power of the Colorado River. Within a couple of days, the two entered President Harding Rapid in Marble Canyon. Beer made it through safely, but Daggett wasn't so lucky. As Beer recalled Daggett's immediate post-Harding comments,

> *I hit my head . . . look, my hand is laid open. Is that bone down there? I went under . . . under the damn rock . . . everything was all tangled up . . . my boxes*

were tangled up [the swimmers were tethered to their
storage boxes] . . . my life jacket was pulling on me. I
was dead. . . . [But] the river jammed me up . . . then
I hit my head . . . see? It's all bloody. It won't stop
bleeding. I didn't have any air.

Beer recognized Daggett's disorientation as a symptom of shock, but there was no place to camp at their landing spot. As it turned out, there was no place to camp for several miles downstream. They both ended up back in the river, floating on in search of a camp. "Thank God John didn't have to move," Beer wrote. "His head and his hand wouldn't stop bleeding. He was just sitting there between his boxes [the two used the storage boxes as pontoons], holding his hand in the air, looking at it bleed and wondering why it wouldn't stop."

They made camp, and after cleaning Daggett's deep finger wound, it became apparent that it was nasty looking but not life threatening. A makeshift splint closed up the finger wound, and they collectively decided to leave the multiple wounds on his head alone— stitches were probably in order, but that, of course, wasn't an option.

Eventually, they made it to the footbridges over the Colorado near Phantom Ranch. They decided to hike out to the rim on the South Kaibab Trail to get some supplies and a good night's sleep. Once on the rim, they found out that search-and-rescue planes were flying over the river corridor looking for the two, and that they had generated quite a bit of media interest as well as the full attention of the National Park Service. Newspaper headlines pronounced them dead, and a flurry of phone calls to family was necessary for the two to set the story straight. They also had to do some fast talking to avoid park service attempts to end their adventure right then and there. In the end, they headed back down the trail, without the official blessing of the park service, but also without rangers forcibly trying to stop them. All of the attention they had generated excited the pair.

Beer and Daggett got back in the water and went on, eventually reaching the landing at Pierce Ferry, an access point to the Colorado River beyond the end of the canyon at the Grand Wash Cliffs.

Beer and Daggett completed their goal, and the intense media attention afterward was icing on the cake. Beer noted in his book (first published in 1988) that thirty years later, when on a commercial raft trip through the canyon with his kids, the river runners that accompanied him called the two "legends." Of course, the only difference between a legend and a forgotten fool at the Grand Canyon is survival.

THE FALLEN

- 1956 -

The whole world is shocked by the collision of two big airliners over northern Arizona Saturday, the worst commercial air disaster in history. . . . The hand of Fate intervened to toss them together, the one chance in probably millions that such an accident could occur.

—PAT CLINE, EDITOR, *ARIZONA DAILY SUN* (FLAGSTAFF), MONDAY, JULY 2, 1956

THE BACKCOUNTRY OF THE GRAND CANYON IS SOME of the most remote and rugged wilderness in the United States. Many areas can only be reached on foot or via the Colorado River, with the inherent buttes, spires, and air currents of the canyon making helicopter landings very difficult. Some areas are wholly inaccessible. Those who make it into the canyon have to contend with intense heat, unrelenting exposure to direct sun, and limited water sources; experienced backpackers avoid hiking in the canyon entirely during the summer. The section of the park north of the Colorado River near the main river's confluence with the Little Colorado River is a case study in difficult-to-access and dangerous wilderness. On June 30, 1956, National Park Service (NPS) rangers, officials of the federal Civil Aeronautics Administration (CAA), the U.S. Air Force, the U.S. Army, Coconino County, and a team of Swiss mountain climbers faced the daunting challenge of a major search-and-rescue operation in this rugged area of the park. At about 11:31 A.M. that day, *two* commercial airliners with 128 passengers and crew on board plummeted from 21,000 feet and crashed near the confluence, painting what a reporter later described as "two black splotches in the buff-colored terrain" of the canyon.

It was not immediately apparent what had happened. The airplanes, Trans World Airlines (TWA) Flight 2, en route from Los Angeles to Kansas City, and United Airlines Flight 718, traveling from Los Angeles to Chicago, were not flying in their original flight channels and should have been flying 2,000 feet apart vertically. A tourist on the South Rim reported seeing a column of smoke in the canyon near the confluence of the two rivers, and United Airlines later released to authorities a recording of the final transmission from Flight 718 with an unknown crewman stating, "We are going—" followed by radio silence. Palen and Henry Hudgin, pilots and owners of Grand Canyon Airlines, positively identified the wreckage of the TWA flight in the canyon early in the evening of June 30; searchers identified the wreckage of the United flight the next morning.

Friends and relatives of the passengers and crew waited patiently at Kansas City Municipal Airport and at Chicago's Midway Airport for the arrival of the planes, as the airlines announced that the planes were "late" and that more information would be forthcoming. Most remained at the airports until officials broke the horrific news of the crashes to them in the late afternoon and early evening.

In Arizona, a search-and-rescue operation took its first steps, with a command center set up at Winslow, east of Flagstaff. Initially, more than one hundred airplanes were involved in the effort, but by Sunday, July 1, with both crash sites identified, the planes were grounded as it became apparent what had happened. "It's almost undoubtedly a collision in flight," search officer Captain Alvin C. Scott told the press. The director of the search-and-rescue operation, Captain Byrd Ryland, agreed, saying the planes "must have" collided in the air. By July 3, after visiting the TWA site, Ryland was able to confirm his suspicions, noting that he had seen paint scratches from the United plane on pieces of the TWA plane.

But were there survivors? Palen Hudgin shared what he had seen while flying over the wreckage on June 30: "The planes were about 1,000 feet apart," Hudgin told authorities and the press. "There should not be much problem bringing bodies out because there will be little remaining." When interviewed fifteen years later for an article on the crashes in *Arizona* magazine, Hudgin was emphatic. "[There was] no possibility of survivors," he said. "Because of the impact and the fire afterward."

As search teams reached the TWA site in the days following the crashes, the scale of the disaster stunned officials. Coconino County Coroner Shelby McCauley was one of the first officials on the ground near the TWA plane. "There were no complete corpses," he told the *Arizona Daily Sun*. "The bodies were in such a condition it was impossible to tell if we had one or two." Officials helicoptered out rubberized bags filled with remains. The remains were transported to the Grand Canyon Airport, then near Red Butte 16 miles south of the park, and they were subsequently flown to Flagstaff aboard an Army transport plane. Attempts at identification were made at a temporary morgue within the Coconino County Fairgrounds.

But only three victims from the TWA flight were ever identified. On Monday, July 9, the remains of the sixty-seven unidentified TWA passengers were laid to rest in a common plot in Flagstaff Cemetery. The front-page photograph of the ceremony that appeared in the (Phoenix) *Arizona Republic* showed sixty-seven coffins in three rows, including a tiny coffin holding the remains of an infant.

After the final remains of victims were removed from the TWA crash site on July 4, officials turned their attention to the much-more-difficult-to-access United crash site—2,600 feet above the floor of the Grand Canyon on Chuar Butte. Professional mountain climbers from Colorado initially worked their way up the butte from the bottom, but an Army helicopter carried the first crews to the scene when it landed on a tiny spot just above the crash site on July 5. They were aided the next day by eight Swiss Air Rescue Patrol mountain climbers, who flew to the Grand Canyon to assist in the recovery effort. Almost immediately, the crews found human remains—and further evidence of a mid-air collision. By July 10, twenty-nine victims of the United crash had been identified. Their remains were returned to their families for burial. On July 12, the remains of the twenty-nine unidentified victims were buried in the Grand Canyon cemetery, during a small ceremony attended by eleven local and airline officials.

On August 2, a second ceremony was held at the Grand Canyon, attended by relatives and friends of the United victims. Officials placed a limestone monument listing thirty-one names (including the twenty-nine unidentified dead and two identified victims whose names relatives requested be included on the monument). A wreath of 2,500 carnations spelling out the Twenty-Third Psalm draped the monument. The monument still stands in the Grand Canyon Pioneer Cemetery, just west of the Shrine of the Ages.

As souls were laid to rest, the investigation into what had happened continued. On August 3, Walter and Blanche England reported to the investigating board what they had seen in the sky while driving on U.S. Route 66 west of Winslow (about 100 miles southeast of the crash site) on June 30. Blanche England recalled: "All at once I saw a great puff of smoke, something came out of the sky like a parachute. Then something came down, with smoke following after it." She said the puff of smoke appeared to be just above a dark thundercloud. Frederick Riley, who was driving near Flagstaff (75 miles south of the crash site) that day, reported seeing two planes come together and then "fly as if stuck together."

Evidence from the crash site confirmed that the two planes had collided. The investigation concluded that the left wing of the United plane had sliced through the fuselage of the TWA plane, lopping off the latter plane's tail and crippling both airliners. Air traffic control records from that day confirmed that the commander of the TWA plane, Captain Jack Gandy, had asked permission to climb from 17,000 feet to 21,000 feet at the California-Arizona border due to thunderclouds. Air traffic controllers denied the request because the United flight was already cruising at 21,000 feet. The TWA pilot then asked permission to fly 1,000 feet "above the weather," a common request at the time that was granted by air traffic controllers. It later became apparent that the top of the weather system was at an elevation of 20,000 feet, meaning the 1,000-foot climb "above the weather" put the TWA plane in the path of the faster United plane. At the time, the request by the TWA flight to gain altitude meant the pilot would be operating under "visual flight rules," meaning the plane was no longer monitored by air traffic controllers, and the TWA pilot had the duty to avoid other aircraft. However, an earlier government report concluded that it was "impossible for a pilot to fly a high-speed, modern airplane effectively without almost continuous reference to his cockpit instruments. Hence under the best conditions, the pilot, even if he is alert, may not be looking out of his airplane when a midair collision is imminent." It seemed that an improbable series of routine events had led to the worst commercial air disaster the world had ever seen.

As a result of the Grand Canyon aircraft crashes, the U.S. Congress passed new laws governing commercial flights, including mandating the formation of the Federal Aviation Administration (FAA), which was granted the authority to regulate the airlines, investigate accidents, and prescribe steps to avoid similar accidents in the future.

At the August 2 memorial for the United victims at the Grand Canyon, the Reverend Hilka Green of the Grand Canyon Community Church spoke to the gathered mourners: "Our small world may be shattered many times, but God's world goes on. Where can we be more conscious of this than in this national park, where through eons of time God's hand has etched out of stone unmatched beauty and wonder?"

THE BATTLE OF EL TOVAR

- 1966 -

DAMMING THE GRAND CANYON OF THE COLORADO RIVER is an older idea than the national park itself. "The eyes of many engineers are on the Grand Canyon and the Colorado River," the (Flagstaff) *Coconino Sun* reported on November 14, 1913, "figuring on the vast possibilities of the great gorge for the development of water and power." Indeed, the Grand Canyon is a perfect place for dams, given its sheer canyon walls and tremendous depth, its powerful river in an arid desert, and its nearly uninhabited landscape. And dreamers in the state capitol saw a chance to create boomtowns in the desert, with water flowing to Phoenix and Tucson on a system of pumps and canals that were financed by the huge profits from sales of dam-created electricity. The canyon, after all, is bookended by two dams: Hoover Dam, completed in 1936, and Glen Canyon Dam, completed in 1964. Damming was "progress" in the Southwest.

In the mid-1960s, the federal government started pushing for legislation that would authorize the construction of two dams in the Grand Canyon. At the time, environmentalists were small in number and weak in political influence, so getting attention for their battle to stop the construction of these dams was extremely difficult. In March 1966, at the South Rim of the Grand Canyon, all that changed.

Beginning in 1963, the federal government actively sought to build a dam at Bridge Canyon, to the west of Grand Canyon Village, and one at Marble Canyon, to the north of Desert View. Secretary of the Interior Stewart Udall (an Arizonan) and Commissioner of the Bureau of Reclamation Floyd Dominy spearheaded the effort. At the time, neither dam site was within Grand Canyon National Park, although water from the lake created by Bridge Canyon Dam could have backed up through then–Grand Canyon National Monument and across the then-boundary of the national park. The idea was part of the Central Arizona Project, a vast public-works super-system purposed with moistening Arizona's deserts for agriculture and development. The project had been debated in Congress, on and off, since the 1940s.

The proposals to build the two dams rose to the surface of Washington politics in 1963, when the U.S. Supreme Court ruled in favor of Arizona in a more than forty-year-old dispute with California over Colorado River water rights. Under the 7–1 ruling (Chief Justice Earl Warren, a California native, abstained), issued on June 3, California had the right to use 4.4 million acre-feet of Colorado River water annually and Arizona had the right to 2.8 million acre-feet. (An acre-foot is equal to the amount of water necessary to cover an acre of land under one foot of water.) In addition, the Gila River, which flows through Arizona to the Colorado, was ruled to not be part of Arizona's Colorado River allotment, which had the effect of giving Arizona an additional million acre-feet of water. The ruling helped define the scope and scale of the

Central Arizona Project, which would involve moving large amounts of water from the Colorado River to southern Arizona. Shortly after the ruling, legislation including the Central Arizona Project and its two Grand Canyon dams was introduced in the U.S. Congress.

Given that the secretary of the interior was an Arizonan, his brother Morris Udall was a congressman from the state, and the senate's senior statesman Carl Hayden also hailed from the Grand Canyon State, the pro-dam political forces seemed to have come together in a "perfect storm" that would allow supporters to hammer through Congress the two canyon dams. The damming of Grand Canyon, in 1963 and for several years thereafter, seemed inevitable.

By the spring of 1966, the legislation, after several starts and fits, had worked its way through the legislative process and was poised for consideration by the House Interior Committee. In January of that year, *Reader's Digest* magazine had agreed to run an anti-dam article written by Sierra Club activist and Cornell physics professor Richard Bradley. With a circulation of some thirty-five million readers across the country, the magazine offered a tall soapbox that had not been available to groups fighting the two dams before. In March 1966, in advance of the publication of the article (slated for April), *Reader's Digest* asked Sierra Club Executive Director David Brower to moderate a symposium on the dams at El Tovar Hotel on the South Rim. Brower agreed, and the El Tovar gathering was scheduled for March 30 and 31.

According to author Byron E. Pearson, in his book *Still the Wild River Runs: Congress, the Sierra Club, and the Fight to Save Grand Canyon* (2002), "*Reader's Digest* intended the event to be a celebration of the publication of Bradley's article and an opportunity for opponents of the dams to present their side without interference from supporters of the project." However, *Reader's Digest* hired an outside firm to stage the event, and a misunderstanding between the two resulted in invitations being sent to prominent pro-dam politicians and government officials. In addition, an airplane was chartered to carry numerous members of the national media to Grand Canyon.

On March 30, according to Pearson, David Brower and Sierra Club Southwest Representative Jeff Ingram took a stroll along the South Rim, happy that the publicity-creating symposium was about to start. But when they returned to El Tovar, they found a huge scale-model of the Grand Canyon, with plastic inserts to show where the Bureau of Reclamation claimed the water from the two new reservoirs would be, plunked in the middle of the hotel's dining room. Now in attendance were several high-powered pro-dam leaders, including Arizona Congressman Morris Udall and Bureau of Reclamation chief Floyd Dominy. As the Sierra Club leaders were not aware of the invitations to pro-dam advocates, the presence of the model, Udall, and Dominy nearly brought the two sides to blows. Only the timely arrival of National Park Service rangers averted the outbreak of widespread fisticuffs in the historic hotel.

Frantic calls to Secretary Udall, *Reader's Digest,* and others eventually led to a truce of sorts. Brower stepped down as moderator and some pro-dam activists would be allowed to speak. The crowd was overwhelmingly against the projects, but with government leaders in attendance to lobby for the dams, Brower and others feared their long-sought national spotlight would be stolen by their opponents.

Indeed, Congressman Udall took to the podium on the night of March 30, and he immediately launched an attack on the anti-dam activists, in an effort to prove their stance ridiculous to the numerous reporters in attendance. Predictably, the largely anti-dam crowd made quite a racket, shouting at and booing the congressman during his remarks. However, dam opponents went to bed that night feeling certain their symposium had been co-opted by dam-loving politicians.

The next morning, things got worse. Former Arizona Senator and Republican nominee for president Barry Goldwater arrived, a mega-wattage hero to American conservatives; predictably, he became an instant camera magnet upon his arrival. At the symposium, Goldwater spoke in strong support of the Bridge Canyon Dam (he seemed less enthusiastic about the Marble Canyon Dam), and, according to Pearson, he dominated the speaking time that morning. After he finished, many members of the national media ducked out of the room.

Despite such powerful opposition, the anti-dam activists managed to score several points during the symposium, including forcing Goldwater to admit the Navajo Nation had not been consulted about Marble Canyon Dam despite the fact that the east anchor for the dam comprised Navajo land. This was a major admission, especially since the pro-dam faction had accused environmentalists of being racist for opposing Bridge Canyon Dam, which would abut Hualapai Indian Reservation land. (The Hualapai—a tiny, remote, impoverished tribe—wanted the dam for economic reasons.) Environmentalists also raised serious questions about why less costly and less damaging options were off the table. They argued that such power sources as a coal-fired steam plant or even a nuclear power plant would provide the cash cow the government sought. (Nuclear power had not yet gained the ire of most environmentalists.)

After the symposium, members of the press were flown over the canyon by helicopter, and Martin Litton, a Sierra Club leader, showed the reporters firsthand what would be flooded from Toroweap Point on the North Rim. The stunning spot features a several thousand foot drop to the Colorado River, and those on the rim can hear the thunderous roar of Lava Falls, likely the most difficult and spectacular rapid in North America. Lava Falls would be drowned by the lake created by Bridge Canyon Dam, and Litton drove this point home to the awestruck journalists.

When the symposium broke up, most anti-dam activists felt the symposium was a bust. Government officials had upstaged them, and in all likelihood, the Grand Canyon dams would be built. But in the end, the demoralized activists were saved by the very canyon they were trying to protect.

As it turned out, the Grand Canyon had wowed reporters, and most returned to their publications and broadcast stations with a feeling of shock that anyone would want to flood such a magnificent American icon. Pro-dam officials countered that the part of Grand Canyon viewable from the South Rim would not be touched by the reservoirs, but their protests were drowned out by the publication and broadcast of anti-dam stories across the country. Soon, most of America was aware of the government's "plan to dam Grand Canyon," and a landslide of letters to representatives in Congress and to President Lyndon Johnson made clear the Battle of El Tovar, as it came to be known, had been won by environmentalists.

After the symposium, the fight over the dams continued. But the El Tovar conference was a turning point in the debate that finally leveled the playing field between the anti-dam activists and government officials. As the summer of 1966 wore on, the bill including the dams continued to move through Congress, but it was stopped in the fall through political maneuvering partially influenced by the outpouring of opposition to the two dams. After the most promising legislation, in the view of dam supporters, stalled, the government moved to drop the dams from the bill. Considerable wrangling ensued, but legislation to create the Central Arizona Project without the Grand Canyon dams emerged from Congress. On September 30, 1968, President Johnson signed the bill. Just before leaving office in January 1969, President Johnson also extended national monument status to Marble Canyon, making it extremely difficult to build a dam there in the future. Six years later, Marble

Canyon National Monument, Grand Canyon National Monument (just to the west of Grand Canyon National Park), and the rest of the Colorado River through the entire Grand Canyon were incorporated into the national park. In 1975, the greatest environmental battle in American history finally ended, and the Grand Canyon was indeed saved for future generations.

LOST

- 1975 -

WILDERNESS DEFINES THE GRAND CANYON. Many think of the canyon as an American icon, like the Statue of Liberty or Mount Rushmore, but unlike those places, the canyon harbors vast wilderness both in the national park and in neighboring areas. The Havasupai Indian Reservation abuts Grand Canyon National Park to the southwest, and on August 1, 1975, Linda Forney, a twenty-five-year-old soft-spoken nurse from Pittsburgh, decided. to hike into Havasu Canyon with Cocoa Gin, her cockapoo, intending to see the reservation's famous waterfalls.

The hike to Supai, the main village on the Havasupai reservation connected only by trail and helicopter to the outside world, is relatively mild by Grand Canyon standards. After several sharp switchbacks below the trailhead, the trail crosses a broad platform and drops into Hualapai Canyon. From there, the trail follows the gently sloping gradient of the wash in the canyon to azure Havasu Creek, which flows alongside the trail another mile or so before reaching

Supai. The campground and Havasu Falls, the most famous waterfall in the canyon, are another 2 miles down the trail. The total distance from the trailhead to Supai is 8 miles.

Hiking the trail in the summertime can be dangerous, given the intensity of the sun, the lack of shade, and the possibility of monsoon-season flash flooding. Hikers are advised to leave very early in the morning to avoid the sun and to minimize the chances of being caught in a flash flood, which are typically triggered by afternoon thunderstorms in July and August.

Forney made several errors at the beginning of her hike, including starting down from the trailhead at noon and dressing in blue jeans and a halter-top, the latter providing little protection from the sun. The heat was unrelenting, topping 100°F as she crossed the treeless plateau and began to descend Hualapai Canyon. It is unclear whether the stifling heat or sun overexposure contributed to Forney's confusion, but when she arrived at Havasu Creek, she turned right instead of left, hiking away from Supai up Havasu Canyon.

Earlier that year, the Havasupai Indians had won a historic battle with the federal government over the boundaries of the Havasupai reservation. Before 1975, the Havasupais had been confined to a tiny reservation of 518 acres at the bottom of Havasu Canyon along the creek. The reservation did not include any of the Havasupais' traditional grazing and hunting lands on the plateaus, the major falls of Havasu Creek, or the campground. The acreage was so small that it was nearly impossible for the roughly 400 Havasupais living there to make a living from farming, one of the tribe's only sources of income. On January 3, 1975, after nearly a century of battle with the federal government, the Havasupais won back 160,000 acres, as well as special-use permits to graze livestock on an additional 95,000 acres of federal land on the plateau. It was the largest return of federal land to a single tribe in American history.

When Forney went right at Havasu Creek, she was still hiking on reservation land and would be for quite some time. But Supai, then as now, is the only town on the reservation, and the newly acquired acreage upriver from Supai was seldom visited. For the next nineteen days, she would be on her own.

As night fell that first day, Forney knew she was lost. Scared, she started screaming, but no one heard her. She soon set her pack down by the side of the trail, thinking she could move quicker to find the village without the excess weight.

"It just started getting very dark," she later told reporters. "I lay down to go to sleep, but I was too scared to sleep."

By the third day in the canyon, she had settled into a routine of traveling only at night and in the early morning, while ducking under trees and overhangs during the day to stay out of the direct sunlight.

"I'd be so cold in the morning, I couldn't wait for the sun to come up," she said. "Then it was so hot I couldn't stand it."

She tried hard to alert somebody, anybody, of her predicament. "For the first four days I tried screaming," she said, "but that didn't help. Your voice doesn't carry that far."

On her third day in the canyon, she found a tiny spring, but it was a mere trickle. She used a hard-shell eyeglass case to catch the water, and she had to hold the case steady for forty-five minutes to fill it each time. Frustrating as this was, that dripping spring undoubtedly saved her life. Later she found an empty glass liquor bottle that she could fill, which allowed her to stray farther from the spring in search of help.

For food she relied almost exclusively on the blossoms and pulp of prickly pear cactus, the latter gouged out of the prickly paddles with a paring knife.

Her dog Cocoa Gin stayed by her side the first two weeks, but on August 14, the cockapoo wandered off. The dog was found later by a couple of hikers, who nursed the dehydrated and emaciated pooch back to health. Cocoa Gin was later reunited with Forney.

Forney wasn't due back at her job in Pittsburgh until August 13, and her family and friends were unaware she was in any danger until she failed to show up for work—twelve days after she had stepped onto the trail at Hualapai Hilltop. It took a few days before those in Pittsburgh figured out where she probably was: somewhere in the slickrock and sheer cliffs of a remote Indian reservation in the Southwest. They notified the Coconino County Sheriff's Department in Flagstaff on August 18.

On August 19, Havasupai Hardy Jones noticed tracks far up Havasu Canyon, "where nobody should be." Unaware of Forney's disappearance, he returned to Supai and told others what he had seen. The next morning, Jones, his son Darryl, Stanley Manakaja, and Roy Young, returned to the site, about 15 miles from town in Havatagvitch Canyon, a side canyon to Havasu Canyon. As they came upon the tracks, they heard a woman's voice calling to them.

"I just started crying," Forney later told reporters. "I went up and hugged one guy. They even had food for me."

Forney was treated at the clinic in Supai and then transferred by helicopter to the Grand Canyon Clinic at the South Rim. Stable enough to travel, she was then driven to Flagstaff Community Hospital. She had lost twenty-one pounds, weighing a mere eighty-five pounds when she was examined.

Her first meal after leaving Havasu Canyon included chicken salad and chocolate ice cream. After spending the night at the Flagstaff hospital, she was released. Forney and her brother Tom, who had flown out from Detroit to join the search party, then began the long car ride home.

AIRBORNE BURROS

- 1980 -

BURROS AND MULES AND THE GRAND CANYON FIT in the public's mind like peanut butter and jelly. Since at least 1886, tourists have ridden sure-footed, floppy-eared mules into the canyon and back out again. They were likely in use by inner-canyon prospectors even earlier. In 1953 Marguerite Henry's book *Brighty of the Grand Canyon* was published, introducing a generation of children to the adventures of a Grand Canyon burro. A bronze statue of Brighty sits in the North Rim Lodge today, and visitors to the South Rim have to slow down for mule crossings.

But in the 1970s, feral, or wild, burros (distinct from the canyon's domesticated mules in that they can reproduce; mules are always the result of breeding a male donkey, or burro, with a female horse) became a major ecological problem in the inner canyon. The burros were the descendants of animals abandoned by miners in the 1880s and 1890s, and although the National Park Service estimated there were only 300 to 500 feral burros in the canyon in the late

1970s, they ate an enormous amount of vegetation, eradicating some plants from entire areas of the national park. And they reproduced quickly, meaning the population was growing rapidly. This was a threat not only to the plants themselves but to animal species that relied on the plants, including desert bighorn sheep.

As the burros were not native to the canyon, and given that the park service is mandated to protect and preserve native species of flora and fauna, the park service had decided in the 1920s that the burros in the canyon would be shot and killed by park service employees. There seemed no reason to change the policy by the late 1970s. Economics, in fact, argued strongly against any change in policy: The park service estimated it would cost $360,000 to capture and fly out the burros, but it would cost only $30,000 to shoot them.

But this time, the news media caught on to the park service's plan. Naturally, the thought of crosshairs being aligned on the braying head of Brighty caused an uproar. It did not matter that the feral burros were a threat to the canyon ecosystem or that the park service and licensed hunters had killed thousands of feral burros in the canyon over the years. It did not matter that the park service was constantly cash-strapped and that choosing an option that cost more than ten times as much as another option was simply not feasible for a government agency.

Luckily for the park service, which was doing the right thing but couldn't convince the public of the benevolence of shooting feral burros, the Fund for Animals stepped in with a plan to trap the animals and fly them out of the Grand Canyon. They would then be placed with carefully screened families.

The park service supported the Fund for Animals' effort, although the government set a sixty-day deadline to remove the burros. After that date, they would be shot. Lawsuits filed by the American Horse Protection Association and the Humane Society of the United States led a judge to extend that deadline until the resolution of the lawsuits. With that ruling, all eyes turned to the Fund for Animals.

"If we can get them out of the Grand Canyon, we can get them out of anywhere," Cleveland Amory, writer and founder of the Fund for Animals, told the media.

However, the Fund for Animals, based in New York City, realized it didn't possess the expertise to round up and airlift hundreds of feral burros out of the Grand Canyon. They contracted out the job to Arizona rancher Dave Ericsson, who had rounded up hundreds of feral burros on Bureau of Land Management land in the late 1970s.

In July 1980 Ericsson and five additional cowboys, twenty-one horses, six Catahoula dogs, and two helicopters, began the roundup. The Catahoula dog, according to Ericsson, "is a rare breed which is particularly adept at herding burros off ledges and other difficult places without injury to dog or burro."

Over and over again, Ericsson and the Fund for Animals emphasized that the operation would be carried out with constant attention to minimizing stress on the burros. Burros would be driven off ledges by the dogs and hobbled, put into a hammock, and then flown, dangling from a cable attached to a helicopter, to an inner-canyon corral. Once the animals had mellowed in their new confines, they would be bundled up again and flown to a corral on the South Rim. From the outside, the idea seemed on par with the 1924 attempted mule deer drive on the North Rim. But, amazingly, the burro roundup worked.

As the television news cameras rolled, burro after burro was flown out dangling in a cargo net, with the Grand Canyon as a majestic backdrop. Hearts melted across America, and donations soared for the Fund for Animals. Interestingly, the park service also received good publicity from the burro airlift, as the details of the whole thing were lost on people amazed at seeing burros flying over the Grand Canyon.

The park service was pleased with the results. "We are carefully monitoring the program carried on by the group but have no complaints," National Park Service Resource Management Specialist Jim Walters told the media. "They are making good progress. We are very grateful to members of the Fund for Animals for their help."

Once on the South Rim, a team of veterinarians examined the animals for disease and stress problems. For the most part, the burros removed from the canyon were healthy and quickly recovered from the trauma of relocation. From the South Rim corral, they were taken to the Fund's Black Beauty Ranch in Texas, home to abused horses and other animals.

After it was all over, the Fund for Animals estimated it had caught, removed, and brought to Texas 580 burros from the Grand Canyon at an estimated cost of $2,000 per burro. The Fund was able to find homes for a little more than 500 of the animals; the remainder lived out their days at the ranch. When the costs were tallied, the operation cost considerably more than the original $250,000 estimate; the total came to more than $1 million. Although this amount nearly equaled the Fund for Animals' annual budget, the publicity over the Grand Canyon project increased donations dramatically, and the organization was able to cover the costs.

Today, a few feral burros remain in the Grand Canyon, mostly in the western areas of the national park.

THE UNDERMINING OF
GLEN CANYON DAM

- 1983 -

GLEN CANYON DAM HOLDS BACK MASSIVE LAKE POWELL just north of Grand Canyon National Park. Completed in 1964, the dam changed the Colorado River in Grand Canyon dramatically, eliminating periodic floods, stopping fluctuating water temperatures (the water that flows from the dam into the river is taken from far below the lake's surface, and the river water in the upper canyon maintains a temperature of roughly 48° F), and siphoning much of the sediment flowing downriver. The changes destroyed beaches, allowed nonnative plant species such as tamarisk to thrive, and killed off or dangerously threatened several native species of fish. And this is not even to mention the loss of glorious Glen Canyon, argued by some to be more beautiful than Grand Canyon, but now submerged under Lake Powell. To put it mildly, Glen Canyon Dam is controversial.

Nineteen years after the completion of the dam, record snowmelt from the Rocky Mountains filled Lake Powell higher than it had ever been before. The top of the dam is at 3,715 feet above sea level, and the openings to concrete-lined spillways (meant to divert water around the dam at times of high lake levels) top out at 3,648 feet above sea level, with an additional 52.5 feet in adjustable gates to manage water flow into the spillways. On June 2, 1983, the water level in Lake Powell reached 3,696 feet above sea level, 4½ feet shy of the top of the adjustable gates guarding the spillways.

The Bureau of Reclamation, which built and operates the dam, saw the danger, and they adjusted the left spillway gate, increasing the flow of water to 20,000 cubic feet per second (cfs) from 10,000 cfs. But after four days of high water flow through the left spillway, engineers heard rumbling deep within the dam and saw chunks of cement and steel girders shooting out of the spillway into the river. Even to nonengineers, this was a bad sign. Acting quickly, the bureau shut down the left spillway and compensated by opening the right spillway and the river outlet works, which routes water to the energy-producing turbines of the dam.

Bureau officials were subsequently lowered into the closed-off left spillway, where they found deteriorating concrete and jagged steel protruding from the walls. This put the engineers in a bit of a pickle because Lake Powell continued to rise, and they had seemingly lost the use of one of the emergency spillways. With few options, the bureau ordered the installation of 4-foot-high sheets of specially designed plywood on top of the spillway gates, giving the engineers a few extra feet to work with.

But the lake continued to rise.

At first, they allowed a water flow of only 4,000 cfs to shoot through the right spillway, because it was positioned in a way that if it deteriorated and the water carved into the soft Navajo sandstone surrounding the spillway, the resulting damage could undermine the dam and allow water to flow freely around the structure. Such a scenario would deluge both the river in the Grand Canyon and Hoover Dam—as well as all of the other dams, several towns, and a lot of farmland downstream—with potentially catastrophic results.

By the middle of June, the total discharge from the river outlet works, the right spillway tunnel, and the left spillway tunnel, which was reopened despite the damage, reached 53,000 cfs—well above the normal 21,000 cfs. Shortly thereafter it became apparent that there was a blockage in the left spillway. The bureau subsequently increased the flow into that spillway with the hope of water-cannoning the obstruction to restore the free flow.

But the lake continued to rise.

By June 22 the total flow reached 70,000 cfs. "What we thought would be normal runoff is now proving to be 191 percent of normal," a spokesperson for the Bureau of Reclamation told the *New York Times* on June 24, describing the flow into Lake Powell behind Glen Canyon Dam.

The commissioner of the Bureau of Reclamation, Bob Broadbent, speaking at a news conference in Las Vegas on June 24, described how things had gotten so bad, "Candidly, our estimate [of the runoff from the mountains] and what came to us and what happened were wrong."

Jeanne Branson, owner of a riverside resort in Parker, Arizona, many miles below Glen Canyon Dam, was not in a forgiving mood when she commented to the (Flagstaff) *Sun* on June 26. "This is what you call a man-made disaster and there's nothing worse than a man-made disaster," Branson said. "The government got permission to build these dams by saying 'We're going to protect you folks from being flooded.' They've done a great job of it, haven't they?" That same day, the National Guard was sent in to Bullhead City, Arizona, and Needles, California, to prevent looting of flooded-out businesses and homes.

The flow below Glen Canyon Dam reached 92,000 cfs—an astonishing 433 percent of normal—the next day.

As the water continued to surge through the dam's waterworks, it began again to trickle out of the damaged left spillway, a signal that water was getting around the blockage. This was a good sign, but it was barely acknowledged by crews on site because of a coinciding bad sign: The whole dam was vibrating.

"This is no safety problem," a Bureau of Reclamation engineer confidently told the *New York Times*. "We're having some concrete problems in our spillways and we're trying to protect them but if push comes to shove we'll use them to their maximum capability. I really don't think circumstances could develop that would jeopard-ize" the structural soundness of the dam.

Downriver in the Grand Canyon, the tremendous volume of water swamped beaches and river campsites, and threatened the pipeline carrying drinking water to the South Rim from Roaring Springs. On June 18, overwhelmed by huge cataracts, a 37-foot motorized raft carrying eleven passengers flipped in Crystal Rapid (25 miles west of Phantom Ranch).

At first, river-running companies were thrilled by the high water flow, as the voluminous Colorado River was fueling fast-moving water and surging adrenaline in customers. "We're . . . look-ing at a once-in-a-lifetime opportunity to experience the Colorado River in its pre-dam majesty," Rob Elliot of outfitter Arizona Raft Adventures told the (Flagstaff) *Sun* on June 26. Before Glen Canyon Dam was completed, the river sometimes topped out at 120,000 cfs, and on rare occasions, the flow rate climbed even higher.

But the companies also recognized the danger to the Colorado River riverside habitats. Elliot added, "In the old days [before the dam] there would be natural replenishment of the sand [in river sandbars critical to many species of wildlife and vegetation and used as campsites by river runners]. What we lose now we will never see again."

On June 25, four boats capsized in Crystal Rapid, with one man from Colorado drowning in the high water. National Park Service helicopters evacuated some ninety people—fifteen with minor injuries—from the area, and rangers began stopping river runners at Phantom Ranch and warning them of the rough water ahead. The park service also closed Crystal Rapid at this time, requiring river runners to portage about a mile around the roiling water.

It soon became apparent that wasn't enough to ensure river safety, though, and on June 29, National Park Service personnel closed the Colorado to river running and began evacuating all river parties by helicopter. More than 150 people were plucked from the river.

On July 2 the right spillway at Glen Canyon Dam coughed and spurted as the left spillway had done, meaning a blockage was holding back the flow of water. The bureau set to work installing steel extensions on both spillways to replace the plywood extensions put in earlier, which would give the engineers another 4 feet.

Once the steel extensions were in place, they shut down the left spillway and entered it to inspect the damage. What they found horrified them. The tunnel was nearly completely blocked with collapsed steel, concrete, and sandstone, and the engineers saw signs that there had been serious erosion through the bedrock toward the dam. This was bad, very bad.

The next day, they shut down the right spillway and entered it. Although the damage in the right spillway was not as severe as in the left, they found significant erosion of the bedrock. Despite this, the engineers were forced to cautiously open both spillways again to light water flow in an effort to stem the rise of the lake, which had finally slowed.

On July 15 Lake Powell peaked at 3,708.4 feet above sea level, a hair's width shy of the top of the steel extensions and within 7 feet of the top of the dam itself. The emergency was over, and Bureau of Reclamation officials set to work repairing the dam works. Winter runoff has not filled the lake as high since, but the events of June 1983 put kinks in the unshakable confidence of humankind's power over nature.

REACHING INTO THE PAST

- 1989 -

MORE THAN A CENTURY AGO, IN 1901, THE FIRST passenger train reached Grand Canyon Village. The completion of an extension of the line from Anita Junction, a small mining community 20 miles south of the rim, to the village made it possible to travel on the Atchison, Topeka and Santa Fe Railway lines from Chicago or Los Angeles (or anywhere else along the line) to the Grand Canyon via the spur line from Williams. This was a vast improvement over the bouncy stagecoach ride from Flagstaff, which was the principal mode of transportation to the South Rim at the time. Eventually, the prestige of the line from Williams to the Grand Canyon led the Santa Fe to market themselves as the "Grand Canyon Line."

But the automobile eventually grew dominant, as was the case across America, in carrying visitors to the South Rim. The railroad survived carrying tourists as well as ore, lumber, and livestock from the numerous mines, timber operations, and ranches along the line, but by the late 1960s, losses were mounting and ridership was declining. By

1967 fewer than 5,000 people chose the railroad to get them to the canyon, and the closure of mines and other commercial ventures sealed the railroad's fate. On July 30, 1968, the last passenger train left Grand Canyon Village for Williams, and just under a year later, freight operations along the line largely ended. A few irregular freight trains traveled to the canyon in the 1970s.

By the early 1980s, the railroad line was in a serious state of deterioration. Ponderosa and pinyon pines grew between the rails, spikes had rusted away en masse, and the roadbed that supported the rails had been undermined by erosion all along the spur. The Atchison, Topeka and Santa Fe applied to the state to abandon the line. After Arizona approved the request in 1983, the railroad contracted with a Phoenix company, Railroad Resources, Inc., to salvage the raw materials of the line (the rails, ties, spikes, switching equipment, etc.). The president of the salvage company, however, saw potential in the line as a tourist railroad. In 1984, after surveying the line, he purchased from the Santa Fe the railroad, the Fray Marcos Hotel and the station in Williams, and additional properties along the tracks.

The line had sat largely unused for some sixteen years, and Railroad Resources had a major project on their hands. Some 20,000 ties needed to be replaced, vegetation blocking the line had to be cut, and the entire roadbed between Williams and the Grand Canyon required reconstruction. While work on the line commenced, the company sought 1920s-era railroad cars, finding what they needed in New Jersey and Oakland, California. But Railroad Resources was unable to secure enough outside investment to pay for construction, and before the first train of a rejuvenated Grand Canyon Railway chugged north from Williams, the company went bankrupt. For a short time, the dreamy image of a historic railroad to the canyon vanished.

One of the investors the company was able to bring into the project took over the last 20 miles of the line when Railroad Resources went belly up. Max Biegert had made his money from two principal companies dealing in the diverse fields of crop dusting and child-care. As with Railroad Resources, Max and his wife, Thelma, who was intimately involved in the Biegert business operations, were unable to secure the money from outside investors needed to rebuild the line. But this time, things did not end there. The Biegerts came up with the $15 million necessary on their own to get the line moving again. They purchased the additional 44 miles of track from Williams to Anita Junction, which had been repossessed by the Santa Fe, and, by January 10, 1989, the Biegerts felt confident enough to hold a press conference at the historic depot in Grand Canyon Village. They announced the reopening of the line on September 17 of that year, eighty-eight years after the first passenger train had arrived at the South Rim.

The goal was ambitious, as a whole lot of work lay ahead to get the Grand Canyon Railway rolling by September. Crews went to work at the end of March, beginning a few miles north of Williams and slowly working their way north. They replaced ties, spikes, and rails; laid new ballast; straightened and leveled the line throughout its length; and rebuilt bridges. The owners sought out vintage steam-powered engines and historic passenger cars. For the steam engines, the company searched far and wide, including investigating locomotives in China, and they finally found appropriate ones in the Midwest. The railroad purchased three steam engines, each built in 1910, from the Lake States Steam Transportation Company in Wisconsin. The company also bought a fourth steam engine, built in 1906, from a private owner in Iowa, and two diesel locomotives from the Santa Fe. Later in the summer, they purchased a fifth steam engine, discovered at the Mid-Continent Railway Museum, also in Wisconsin.

While workers toiled on the Grand Canyon line during the spring and summer of 1989, the railroad chose seven of the passenger cars for a complete overhaul, as they were in an advanced state of disrepair after years of idleness. The Pacific Fruit Express Company in Tucson took on this project, removing everything in the cars' interiors and sandblasting multiple paint jobs from the exteriors. Workers then repainted the cars and refurbished or replaced everything inside, from new windows to reupholstered seats to refinished wooden sashes and other decorative features. The gleaming, smooth-rolling cars arrived in Williams on September 10.

The railroad picked one of the steam engines, the one in the best condition, for the September 17 run, but the engine didn't arrive at the Williams locomotive works until August 20. In less than a month, workers had to strip down and rebuild the old locomotive, as well as make significant repairs, repaint the engine, and convert the machine from coal to cleaner burning oil. Work on the engine continued nearly around the clock, and workers finished the last details early in the morning of September 17.

Realizing that the steam engine did not have enough power to haul the seven passenger cars needed to carry all of the dignitaries and invited guests expected for the historic run, the railroad decided in September to hook the two former Santa Fe diesel locomotives to the back of the train; they would push from the rear, giving the 1910 workhorse a little help.

The railroad also remodeled the historic Williams train station and Fray Marcos Hotel (a larger, new hotel by the same name would soon be built next to the station and original hotel), and 10,000 people gathered at the station on September 17, 1989, at noon, to watch a rejuvenated Grand Canyon Railway train leave the station. Any doubts about the line's financial survival disappeared after the final tally of passengers for 1990, the first full year of the Grand Canyon Railway's operation, topped 100,000 people.

The railroad continues in operation today, delivering passengers efficiently and comfortably to the national park while keeping an estimated 80,000 cars out of the park every year. By reaching into the past to restore a historic railroad, the Grand Canyon Railway has created a memorable trip to the park for millions of canyon visitors and has helped reduce automobile pollution in one of the crown jewels of the National Park System. It seems fitting, somehow, at this ancient place with its century-old Historic District to have steam engines pulling vintage cars to within a couple hundred yards of what the Santa Fe marketed as the "Titan of Canyons."

DANNY RAY HORNING

- 1992 -

THE GRAND CANYON IS A GOOD PLACE TO GO IF you don't want to be found. Although most tourists to Grand Canyon National Park spend the majority of their time in Grand Canyon Village or at one crowded overlook after another, the Grand Canyon is one of the largest wilderness areas in the country.

Prison inmate Danny Ray Horning was intimately familiar with the northern Arizona backcountry and was trained in wilderness survival during an eleven-month stint in the U.S. Army. On May 12, 1992, Horning, disguised as a medical technician, walked out of the Arizona State Prison at Florence (southeast of Phoenix), where he had been serving four life sentences for bank robbery, kidnapping, and aggravated assault. Almost immediately, he put his survival and criminal skills to work evading authorities in the largest manhunt in Arizona history. And for a time, he repeatedly disappeared and resurfaced in and around Grand Canyon National Park.

After his escape, Horning broke into a cabin near the prison and stole a .44 Magnum, which he subsequently used to rob a bank in

Tucson. Cash and guns are the ingredients for a life on the lam, and Horning, now with both, disappeared. His mug shot was sent to law enforcement units all over the state

Nary a soul saw neither hide nor hair of Danny Ray Horning until June 3, when a U.S. Forest Service employee near the Blue Ridge Reservoir, 60 miles southeast of Flagstaff in the Coconino National Forest, recognized the fugitive. Just as mysteriously as he had reappeared, he again vanished.

In the early days of the manhunt for Horning, his antics attracted some sympathy from the general public, who evidently enjoyed an underdog story. Horning stoked these feelings by sometimes leaving notes apologizing, somewhat, for his dastardly deeds.

Inside a cabin near Pine, Arizona, about 75 miles south of Flagstaff, he opened up the back of the owner's 1980 four-wheel-drive Ford pickup and piled in a .22-caliber rifle, a chain saw, a thirteen-inch color TV, an electric razor, food, sleeping bags, and a toolbox, all of which he swiped from the cabin. He then went to the cabin next door and helped himself to dress clothes, shoes, and a rug, leaving behind an "I'm sorry" note. Then he fled.

"Hell, if he were here, I'd probably give him a beer," a vacationing Phoenix resident in the Coconino National Forest told the *Arizona Daily Sun*.

"He seems like my kind of guy," a tourist from Kingman, Arizona, told the newspaper. On June 25, the *Daily Sun* even ran an editorial under the headline "D. R. Horning: hero or heel?" that debated the mixed feelings many northern Arizonans had for this seeming gentleman bandit. "Horning's popularity has been accentuated by the fact that since his escape, he apparently hasn't hurt a soul," the newspaper wrote.

Temporarily caught up in an exciting game of cops and robbers, many following the story with rising adrenalin found themselves

quietly pleased when Horning eluded authorities. Much to the annoy-
ance of law enforcement officers searching for Horning, the escaped
convict would please the public many times over in the days to come.

On June 21, an Arizona Department of Public Safety officer
spotted Horning in the Ford near Mormon Lake, 20 miles southeast
of Flagstaff. The officer pursued Horning, but the escapee turned off
on rough backcountry forest service roads, and the officer, driving a
Ford Mustang, was unable to keep him in sight. A short time later,
the officer and backup police found the abandoned pickup truck in
the forest. That night, some sixty officers from various law enforcement organizations, as well as several snuffly bloodhounds, searched
the forest around the truck, but they eventually lost the trail. It
became apparent to police that Horning was doubling back over his
tracks and running in figure eights to confuse the dogs. It worked.

In the truck, authorities found another note penned by the
escapee, describing himself as a "freedom fighter" and apologizing to
the owner of the truck. "I am sorry I had to do this to you," Horning wrote. "I am sure you are a nice guy and didn't deserve anything
like this." He also asked to be kept in the truck owner's prayers, noting, "I have a rough road ahead, and could use all the help I can get."

"Anything that happens in the county, Horning's a suspect,"
Coconino County Deputy Sheriff Bill Pribil told reporters on June
25, after an unidentified man fired shots at a National Park Service
police officer who pulled over a truck at Grand Canyon (on West
Rim Drive—today Hermit Road—near Mohave Point). The driver
fled on foot, and the officer found a frightened couple from Flagstaff
sitting in the truck.

The couple was not injured, and they were able to fill in some
holes for law enforcement officials. On the evening of June 24, the
couple had come out of a veterinary clinic on Route 66 in Flagstaff
and found Horning in the parking lot, nudging them toward their

car with his gun. Heading west on Interstate 40, the fugitive and his kidnapped cohorts drove to Kingman, in the northeastern part of Arizona near the Nevada border. They then turned around and drove back to Williams, 30 miles west of Flagstaff and 60 miles south of Grand Canyon. In Williams, Horning forced the couple to withdraw $1,500 from their bank account, which he stuffed into his pockets. They then got back in the car and drove to the national park.

Amazingly, once at the park, the trio checked into El Tovar Hotel and spent the night. The next day they went shopping at Babbitt's General Store in the park, where they stocked up on supplies, including a pair of hiking boots for Horning. Neither the hotel employees nor the sales clerks recognized the fugitive.

The couple told police Horning had said he wanted to go to Grand Canyon in order to kidnap and hold for ransom a "family with a recreational vehicle." The ransom was to be $1 million, freedom for himself, and a get-out-of-jail-free card for his brother, who was also in prison at Florence serving a twenty-nine-year sentence for sexual misconduct with a minor. True to his word, the next evening Horning attempted to kidnap a family in the parking lot of Babbitt's. One of the children started to scream, and Horning, suddenly unnerved, ran back to the car. He opened fire on a National Park Service ranger who had driven over to see what the commotion was about, but the officer was not injured. Nevertheless, Horning sped off with his two hostages. By the time the hostages were found later that night, they had been with Horning for twenty-eight hours.

After the initial Grand Canyon sighting, agents and officers from the Coconino and Gila County sheriff's departments, the FBI, the U.S. Border Patrol, the Navajo Police, and the Department of Corrections descended on Grand Canyon Village in search of their slippery escapee. At the height of the Grand Canyon search, 385 law enforcement officials combed the national park. The wait to get *out* of the park, now hampered by police checkpoints, reached two hours.

On the morning of June 26, Horning turned up yet again, this time hiking down the Bright Angel Trail, shirtless. At least two people noticed him, one waiting for a mule ride at the trailhead and the other a hiker on the trail. Law enforcement officials swarmed over the rim and down multiple trails from the South Rim in pursuit, and a U.S. Border Patrol helicopter with infrared technology made repeated sweeps over the inner canyon, but the officials could not locate the escapee. By June 29, they had returned the focus of their search to the Grand Canyon Village area on the South Rim.

That night Horning surfaced again near Buggeln Picnic Area on East Rim Drive (today Desert View Drive), this time attempting to kidnap an Oregon couple on vacation. The couple managed to get away from Horning, and he took off with their yellow 1978 Chevy station wagon. Surprised campers later spotted him speeding down a forest service road outside of Tusayan, just south of the national park.

The next day, the yellow car turned up, smashed into a tree near Grandview Point on East Rim Drive. Investigators concentrated their search in the area, but Horning was nowhere to be found.

After another sighting and fruitless search on July 2, officials clamped down by closing the South Rim area and not allowing anyone to enter or leave the national park. Given the tremendous number of people this affected heading into the Fourth of July weekend, officials allowed people to come and go through checkpoints when the clampdown yielded no sign of Horning.

Although police did not know it at the time, Horning was on the move. On the morning of July 4, he kidnapped another couple at gunpoint, this time at Desert View, 24 miles east of Grand Canyon Village near the east entrance to the national park. Somehow, they managed to get through two checkpoints, possibly because Horning had bleached his brown hair to a strawberry blond. At one check-point, Horning was even asked to step from the car and remove the straw hat he was wearing, but the officer, not recognizing him, waved the car through. At Red Lake, about 50 miles south of Grand Canyon, Horning pulled over and tied his hostages to a tree. After he fled, the two were able to free themselves and call police.

A Department of Public Safety officer spotted Horning headed south on Interstate 17 toward Phoenix shortly thereafter. A high-speed chase ensued with an exchange of gunfire, but Horning exited the highway and drove the car into a tree, taking off yet again on foot and vanishing.

"It's frustrating," Coconino County Sheriff Joe Richards told reporters after Horning's latest escape. "But I offer no apologies—we've done everything we can." Unknown to the sheriff, the end of Horning's elaborate game of cat and mouse was near.

On July 5, residents in the village of Oak Creek near Sedona saw Horning getting a drink from the garden hose in their yard. The alerted authorities arrived soon thereafter, and this time the blood-hounds led them right to Horning, curled up under a deck, sound asleep. He was arrested without incident.

Horning was charged with four counts of kidnapping, three counts of attempted murder, three counts of attempted kidnapping, and two counts of armed robbery. Bail was set at $2 million, although even if Horning could have raised such a sum, he wouldn't have been freed due to his history of escaping from prison and flight from law enforcement.

Horning was later tried and convicted of a murder in California, a crime for which he was wanted for questioning during his fifty-four day tour of Arizona. His victim had been gruesomely dismembered; Horning was sentenced to death. Other than minor cuts and bruises, no one was injured or killed during the murderer's Grand Canyon crime spree.

TWO BAD DAYS

- 2000 -

MAYBE IT'S NOT THAT HARD TO GET AWAY WITH MURDER, if you're so inclined. By the mid-1990s, three of Robert Spangler's wives had died: one in an apparent suicide, one in a tragic fall from Horseshoe Mesa in the Grand Canyon, and one from a drug overdose. In addition, Spangler's two children were dead, both shot, allegedly by their suicidal mother, just before she shot herself.

That's a lot of tragedy for one man to endure, but those who knew Spangler saw little to indicate either a violent nature or a man burdened by supremely bad luck. He was an Iowa native who had married his high-school sweetheart, an avid Grand Canyon hiker married to a woman who had written a guidebook to hiking the canyon backcountry, a country-music radio deejay, and a referee for kids' soccer and basketball games. His boss at the radio station found little to criticize in his former employee, except to say, "He was too cheerful too early in the morning."

On December 30, 1978, investigators from the Arapahoe County (Colorado) Sheriff's Office, alerted by a neighbor, discovered the bodies of Spangler's wife, Nancy, and his two teenaged children, Susan and David, in the Spangler family's home in Littleton, Colorado. Nancy was found slumped over a typewriter with a suicide note in the carriage; a .38-caliber handgun lay a few feet away, and she had a bullet wound in her upper forehead. Deputies found Susan in her bed with a bullet wound in the back. Her brother, similarly, lay in his bed with a gunshot wound to the sternum.

Robert Spangler returned to his home five hours after the arrival of sheriff's deputies. When an entire family turns up dead except for one member, that person is naturally a suspect, and Spangler was questioned. His alibi was rather simple: He had been at work. He admitted that he and his wife had been having marital problems, and even that he planned to leave her. The .38-caliber pistol belonged to Spangler, and investigators found gunpowder residue on his hand. No such residue was detected on Nancy Spangler. He submitted to two separate, independent polygraph tests, both of which came back "inconclusive."

However, four days after the murders, the county coroner ruled the deaths a double homicide/suicide. Without further evidence and with the official cause of death seemingly exonerating Robert Spangler, the investigation was closed. What little evidence there was was returned to Spangler or destroyed.

As became known to investigators later, Spangler was having an affair with Sharon Cooper at the time his family died. In July 1979, seven months after the death of his family, Spangler and Cooper married.

Robert and Sharon Spangler shared a passion for hiking and rafting in the Grand Canyon. Sharon Spangler even wrote a book about canyon hiking, *On Foot in the Grand Canyon: Hiking the Trails of the South Rim,* first published in 1986. In the acknowledgments to the second edition of the book, published in 1989, Sharon noted, "First, I thank the folks who hiked with me and helped me to see the Grand Canyon through their eyes as well as my own. My husband, Bob Spangler, took photographs, helped me to remember things, encouraged me through the rough times, and, being an accomplished writer, offered suggestions to make the text read better." The couple shared a love of the outdoors, and took long trips together on the canyon's many trails and down the Colorado River.

But as the 1980s began to wind down, so did the Spanglers' marriage. For whatever reason, the couple divorced in 1988 and went their separate ways.

Robert Spangler apparently didn't much like the single life, as he ran a personal ad in a Denver weekly in 1989 that attracted Donna Sundling, a fifty-four-year-old bookkeeper, divorced mother of five, and grandmother of five. The two hit it off, and in 1990, Donna became Spangler wife number three. They moved to Durango, Colorado, the next year, and Robert began work as a part-time country music deejay and volunteer referee, enjoying a semiretirement that allowed him plenty of free time for his beloved Grand Canyon hikes. Donna found work as an aerobics instructor at the Durango Sports Club.

Spangler's new wife didn't necessarily share his love of hiking the canyon. "She was afraid of heights," her former boss at the health club said. "She was real leery of going to the Grand Canyon." But her husband eventually got her to agree to a canyon hike with him, and they set off for Arizona in April 1993.

The two planned to descend the Grandview Trail to Horseshoe Mesa, a U-shaped butte towering hundreds of feet above the inner canyon's Tonto Platform (a broad shelf just above the surging Colorado

River in the dark and foreboding Inner Gorge). The hike down the Grandview is not a particularly brutal one, although it is considerably steeper and rockier than the much more heavily traveled Corridor trails, such as the Bright Angel and the South Kaibab. Tough on the knees, the rapid descent mercifully ends after a mere 3 miles, dropping backpackers off on Horseshoe Mesa. A backcountry campground, partially shaded by squat pinyon pines and junipers, provides the accommodations in this part of the Grand Canyon.

In the Grand Canyon, springs are most common at the base of the Redwall Formation—a sheer, porous cliff of limestone stained red by eroding minerals from the Supai layer just above. Horseshoe Mesa sits atop the Redwall, and it therefore has no water. Backpackers at the campground either need to carry enough with them when they come down the Grandview, or descend an extremely steep trail to Page (Miners) Spring to fill up.

As Robert Spangler later told a ranger on the South Rim, he and his wife had stopped near the top of the trail to Page Spring to take a photograph. Spangler said he was adjusting the camera on its tripod, and when he turned around, his wife was gone. He had heard nothing.

Search-and-rescue rangers recovered Donna Spangler's body 140–160 feet below Horseshoe Mesa, lodged against a tree at the base of a steep slope. Her backpack and one hiking pole sat atop the mesa, while two hats, a second pole, and a pair of glasses littered the slope. A later autopsy report documented "massive injuries, including abrasions, contusions, lacerations, and multiple fractures of the neck, chest, and lower extremities." With injuries consistent with a fall and with her husband's story backing that theory up, Donna Spangler's death was ruled accidental. At the time, investigators looking into the death from the Coconino County Sheriff's Department, National Park Service, and Federal Bureau of Investigation did not know of the deaths of Spangler's first wife and his two children, or that the "unlucky" hiker had been a suspect in that case.

After Donna Spangler's horrible death in 1993, Robert Spangler's second wife, Sharon Spangler, moved back in with the man she had divorced five years earlier. Although she seemed the lucky wife, having left marriage with Robert Spangler alive, her stay with her ex-husband proved quite short. On October 2, 1994, a year and a half after Donna Spangler's death, Sharon Spangler died of a drug overdose. Investigators later concluded that the second Mrs. Spangler died as a result of either suicide or an accident.

After Sharon Spangler's death in 1994, investigators in Arapahoe County reopened the 1978 Spangler case and attempted to interrogate Robert Spangler anew, but this time the three-time widower didn't cooperate, and the case went cold due to lack of evidence.

In January 1999 investigators from several federal agencies and the counties of Coconino in Arizona and Arapahoe in Colorado finally connected the dots and opened an investigation of Robert Spangler in the deaths of his first wife and children, and of his third wife in the Grand Canyon.

"When we got into it a little further," undersheriff of Arapahoe County Grayson Robinson told the *Durango Herald*, "we had reason to believe [the deaths] weren't a coincidence. Frankly, it was just too many people that died [who were] associated . . . with this man."

In 2000 the investigators interviewed a friend of Spangler, who showed them a letter the murder suspect wrote in which he told her he had terminal cancer. A subsequent review of his medical records by a doctor confirmed the diagnosis.

Deciding that there was no time to continue searching for evidence, investigators decided to approach Spangler, request an interview, and see if they could get a confession. The interview took place at the Arapahoe County Sheriff's office. The interrogators told Spangler that the FBI wanted to study him because he was a "unique killer," and this apparently stroked the ego of the suspect. Investigators confronted Spangler with the deaths of his first wife and children, the overdose of his second wife, and the Grand Canyon death of his third wife, and Spangler reacted by saying, "You're naming one too many." Indeed, investigators determined the overdose death of his second wife was not caused (overtly) by Spangler.

By the second day of the interrogation, Spangler perhaps decided he had nothing left to lose, and it was time to come clean. More likely, he wished to brag a little about his actions given that he was dying anyway. Regardless of the reasons, Robert Spangler confessed to shooting Nancy Spangler, Susan Spangler, and David Spangler, although he added that his son required a little smothering with a pillow when the shot to the sternum failed to finish him off. He told investigators that he had fallen in love with another woman (Sharon Cooper), and that killing his family "was simply easier than a divorce."

Investigators pressed for more, and Spangler eventually confessed to shoving Donna Spangler off Horseshoe Mesa in the Grand Canyon, as she faced him at the base of the Grandview Trail on that April day. Interestingly, Spangler had married his fourth wife in September 2000, just before his October confessions.

Spangler was quite concerned about how these confessions would look, and he assured investigators he had lived an upstanding life with many examples of active community involvement, and it was only on one day in 1978 and one day in 1993 that he did "terrible things." He later wrote a letter to an FBI investigator, asking him to keep the case quiet to protect his reputation. Of course, such a wish was quite naïve; the confessions of Robert Spangler made headlines across the country.

"His two bad days deprived four people of thousands of days of life," Undersheriff Robinson told the *Durango Herald*. "I don't have a whole lot of sympathy for him."

Spangler pleaded guilty to first-degree murder for the Grand Canyon death of his third wife. He was sentenced to life in prison without the possibility of parole. Donna Spangler's children sued Spangler and his fourth wife, Judy, for the couple's home in Grand Junction, Colorado, which had belonged to their mother. They won their case. Spangler was not charged in the 1978 murders because of his declining health, although, as noted, he did confess to the crimes.

Robert Spangler died as a result of cancer while incarcerated in federal prison.

FLEDGLING SUPERSTAR

- 2003 -

Endangered didn't really fit the state of California condors in the early 1980s; "one foot in the grave" might have been a better categorization. In 1982 twenty-two California condors were left in the wild, all in California. Although condors had lived in northern Arizona for thousands of years, the last sighting of a wild California condor in the state had occurred in 1924, near Williams, 60 miles south of Grand Canyon National Park. In the dark days of the 1980s, it was hard to be optimistic that these majestic birds with their 9-foot wingspans and bald, wrinkly heads would survive as a species.

Drastic measures were in order. A program with the goal of captive breeding and eventually releasing California condors began in 1982, and in 1987, the last wild condor, known as AC-9, was captured in California. For the first time in thousands of years, no California condors flew in the wild.

The program progressed splendidly, however. The first chick conceived by captive parents hatched in 1988, and more and more chicks hatched in the years that followed. By 1992 the condor population numbered sixty-three, nearly triple what it had been a decade earlier.

With such steady progress, biologists prepared for the reintroduction of California condors to the wild. The first two birds were released in January 1992 at the Sespe Condor Sanctuary in California, with many more releases to follow.

Biologists conducted their work according to the California Condor Recovery Plan, which called for establishing populations in three distinct locations: California, an area separate from California that lay within the condor's historic range, and captivity. Northern Arizona is one of the areas where the condor had historically lived, and researchers knew by the time of the 1992 California releases that the next releases would occur there. The area was nearly perfect for condors: a huge wilderness with relatively few people, many caves available for nesting in the Grand Canyon, and abundant food sources in the forested rim areas and in the canyon. By 1995, officials had chosen a release location at the Vermilion Cliffs, northeast of the national park. The 1,200-foot-high cliffs are remote, border on large areas of federal land, are relatively easy for research teams to access, and offer many ledges far above the ground and well below the cliff edge, perfect places for condors to perch out of reach of predators.

The Arizona reintroduction efforts involved many organizations, with the Peregrine Fund executing the releases. In October 1996 biologists flew with six condors from Burbank, California, to Page, Arizona. Greeted in Page by a gaggle of photographers and reporters, the six celebrities were then flown 25 miles by helicopter to the top of the cliffs, where they were transferred to a large release pen to await their freedom.

As they acclimated to their surroundings, excitement mounted across northern Arizona. When release day finally came on December 12, hundreds gathered below the release site to be present for the historic release. The crowd included Secretary of the Interior Bruce Babbitt, a native Arizonan; Senator John McCain; and Governor Fife Symington. Looking up toward the cliffs with binoculars and spotting scopes, the crowd waited for the condors to take flight. All six birds stepped from the pen, took a look around and down from their lofty launch ramp, stretched out their wings, and took to the skies.

As the years went by, additional releases filled the northern Arizona skies with condors, particularly near the South Rim. According to biologist Sophie Osborn, author of *Condors in Canyon Country: The Return of the California Condor to the Grand Canyon Region* (2007), condors gather en masse in the skies above and the cliffs below the developed area of Grand Canyon Village. They do this, though, not due to a dangerous lack of wariness toward unpredictable humans, but by instinct. The more activity and the longer they linger, the more likely the scavengers will be present when one of the many drops dead or is taken out by a predator, perhaps a less than comforting thought to awestruck visitors with heads craned skyward at the spectacular birds. There is no place in northern Arizona with more activity and larger human "herds" than the South Rim of Grand Canyon National Park.

Through heroic efforts by Peregrine Fund and National Park Service biologists, condors were thriving in northern Arizona by 2003. But all California condors in the wild in both Arizona and California had hatched in captivity; to date, no reintroduced condor pair had successfully raised a chick until fledging (flying away from the nest cave). Condors had laid eggs in nests in the Grand Canyon and in the Vermilion Cliffs in the years just prior to 2003, but none hatched. The failure to hatch a chick disappointed biologists, but they also knew that condors rarely succeeded in hatching a chick on their initial breeding attempts. Although California had had condors successfully hatch chicks, none of the young condors survived to fledging.

In early spring 2003, condors laid three eggs in the Grand Canyon, equaling the number laid in 2001 and 2002 combined. One of the eggs was broken within a week, and another probably did not survive the hatching process, although biologists didn't know this for several weeks—until they were able to rappel down to the nest high in the Redwall cliffs of the canyon. All hopes turned to the third egg, which had been laid in a cliff cave overlooking the Salt Creek drainage in the canyon west of Grand Canyon Village.

Unlike other nest sites, the cave was not viewable from the South Rim. Biologists and volunteer nest watchers had to hike 12 miles each way from the rim to the drainage, where the nest cave opening could be observed through spotting scopes or binoculars. According to Osborn, Grand Canyon National Park condor biologist Chad Olson made the first of many hikes to the drainage on March 14, 2003.

As researchers could not see inside the cave from the drainage, they had to make educated guesses about what was going on inside based on the parents' activities. By June, to the surprised euphoria of many, researchers felt certain the first chick had hatched in Arizona based on observing these activities.

Olson and Osborn hiked into the Salt Creek drainage in mid-August 2003 with the hope of visually confirming the existence of the Grand Canyon chick. To the delight of the condor researchers, they clearly spied through binoculars a four-month-old, black-feathered condor chick in the mouth of the Redwall cave. It was a historic moment for the condor program: the two confirmed the hatching of a condor chick in Arizona for the first time in at least eighty years.

Dubbed Condor 305 by biologists, the Grand Canyon chick continued to develop in the fall of 2003. Volunteers and researchers kept a constant vigil, but Condor 305 obliviously stayed put in the nesting cave. On November 3, Olson and Osborn rendezvoused at the Salt Creek drainage, Olson having hiked over from Phantom

Ranch where he had disembarked from a Colorado River trip through the upper portion of the Grand Canyon. They settled in for their latest shift-keeping vigil.

In the early afternoon of November 5, as Osborn describes in her book, Condor 305 flapped around the entrance to the cave, as he had done on numerous occasions in the past. "Just as it seemed like he was finally winding down at 1:39 P.M.," Osborn writes, "305 craned his neck, looked fixedly at an imaginary ledge, and leaped toward it. [We] shot to our feet. 'He's fledging! He's fledging!' we yelled." The moment of euphoria turned to horror as the chick plummeted toward the ground like a bag of marbles. Then, just before he would have hit the ground, he spread his wings and softly landed at the base of the cliff.

"He didn't move. We didn't move," Osborn writes. "Minutes passed. And then, Condor 305 did what any self-respecting young condor would do: Reaching over to a banana yucca a few inches away, he opened his bill, clamped on, and gave it several sharp tugs. [We] burst out laughing." Success at last.

In the spring of 2004, Condor 305, the first condor to fledge in the wild since 1982, soared out of the Salt Creek drainage and joined his fellow condors in the skies above the Grand Canyon. Chad Olson and Sophie Osborn made their own "condor pair," marrying in the spring of 2006.

GRAND CANYON FACTS & TRIVIA

Grand Canyon National Park is about the size of the state of Delaware.

The white-tailed, tassel-eared Kaibab squirrel lives only on the North Rim of Grand Canyon National Park and in the neighboring North Kaibab Ranger District of the Kaibab National Forest.

Grand Canyon is the fourth-largest national park in the United States outside of Alaska. Only Yellowstone, Death Valley, and Everglades national parks are larger.

Major John Wesley Powell named the Grand Canyon during his second voyage on the Colorado River through the canyon in 1872.

Grand Canyon National Park is the second most-visited park in the United States. Only Great Smoky Mountains National Park in North Carolina/Tennessee receives more visitors.

In 1927, the Clyde Eddy expedition boated through the Grand Canyon planning to film their adventure. The crew included Cataract, a black bear cub from the New York Zoo, and Rags, a "mostly Airedale" hound from the Salt Lake City pound. They became the first bear and the first dog to run the Colorado River in Grand Canyon.

Grand Canyon is one of the Seven Natural Wonders of the World, along with such places at Mt. Everest in Nepal, Australia's Great

Barrier Reef, and Victoria Falls on the border of Zambia and Zimbabwe in Africa.

The rock layers at Grand Canyon range from 270 million years old (more than three times as old as dinosaurs) at the rim to 1.84 billion years old (half as old as the Earth itself) in parts of the Inner Gorge.

The Grand Canyon is approximately six million years old, much younger than its rock walls. The Colorado River cut into the Colorado Plateau and carried away eroded rock to create the Grand Canyon.

Tourists have ridden mules into the Grand Canyon since at least 1886.

In the 1950s, Merle Emery, Beal Masterson, and George Steinke attempted to mine bat guano, which makes good fertilizer, from a cave in western Grand Canyon. As it was expensive and difficult to fly out, the trio sold the guano mining rights, and the company that bought them built a tramway into the canyon and sucked the guano out of the cave with a vacuum hose. The guano ran out after a few years, and the mine was closed.

The Colorado River runs 277 miles through Grand Canyon National Park, just slightly longer than the drive from Grand Canyon Village to Las Vegas, Nevada.

The Colorado River drops in elevation at a rate of 10 feet per mile along its 1,450-mile length. In contrast, the Mississippi River, America's longest river at 2,340 miles, drops at a rate of less than one foot per mile.

In 1999, Robbie Knievel, son of Evel Knievel, jumped a narrow, shallow side canyon of Grand Canyon on his 500-cc motorcycle. In 1968, his father had been denied the chance to jump over the canyon aboard a rocket-propelled motorcycle. The younger Knievel's stunt on the Hualapai Indian Reservation attracted a lot of media attention, but Hualapai tribal member Allan Smith sized up the side canyon noting, "This is barely a wash in this country."

American Indians inhabited or traveled through the Grand Canyon region as long as 12,000 years ago.

Between December 3 and December 7, 1967, a powerful storm dumped more than a foot of rain on the North Rim of Grand Canyon, causing severe flash flooding in Bright Angel Canyon and other inner-canyon areas. The floods damaged the pumphouse at Roaring Springs and the brand-new transcanyon water pipeline, destroyed large sections of the North Kaibab Trail, and swept away several buildings at Phantom Ranch. The debris from the flash flooding created Crystal Rapid on the Colorado River.

The Grand Canyon has an average depth of 1 mile, a little more than four times as tall as the Empire State Building.

The first automobile arrived at Grand Canyon in 1902. The trip from Flagstaff took five days. At the time, a stagecoach ride from Flagstaff took about twelve hours, and today, the drive is about one and one-half hours.

Politicians in Washington, D.C., first discussed making the Grand Canyon a national park in 1882. In 1892, President Benjamin Harrison created the Grand Canon Forest Reserve, the first federal protection of the area. President Theodore Roosevelt created the Grand Canyon National Game Preserve in 1906 and Grand Canyon

National Monument in 1908. The area finally became a national park in 1919.

Eleven American Indian tribes have ties to the Grand Canyon: the Havasupai, Hopi, Hualapai, Kaibab-Paiute, Las Vegas Paiute, Moapa Paiute, Navajo, Utah Paiute, San Juan Southern Paiute, Yavapai-Apache, and Zuni.

Grand Canyon National Park borders three Indian Reservations, two national monuments, two districts of a national forest, and two national recreation areas.

In 1857 the federal government transported several camels and their Arab handlers to northern Arizona. Their mission was to find a wagon road route through the region. The railroad later followed the path the camels trailblazed, as did Route 66 and parts of Interstate 40.

BIBLIOGRAPHY

"2 Men in Copter Reach UAL Wreck." *Arizona Republic* (Phoenix), July 6, 1956.

"29 Buried Today at Grand Canyon." *Arizona Republic* (Phoenix), July 12, 1956.

"29 DC-7 Dead Identified; Mass Services to Be Held for 29 Others in Canyon Crash." *New York Times,* July 11, 1956.

"29 UAL Dead Laid in Canyon Plot." *Arizona Republic* (Phoenix), July 13, 1956.

"67 Crash Victims Buried in Arizona." *New York Times,* July 10, 1956.

"67 Victims of Canyon Air Disaster Rest in Common Grave at Flagstaff." *Arizona Republic* (Phoenix), July 10, 1956.

Adams, Eilean. *Hell or High Water: James White's Disputed Passage through Grand Canyon, 1867.* Logan, Utah: Utah State University Press, 2001.

"Air Victims Remembered in Monument." *Arizona Republic* (Phoenix), August 3, 1956.

"All 128 on 2 Airliners Found Dead; Craft Presumed to Have Collided Before Crashing in Grand Canyon." *New York Times,* July 2, 1956.

Amundson, Michael A. "Mining the Grand Canyon to Save It: The Orphan Lode Uranium Mine and National Security." *Western Historical Quarterly* 32, no. 3 (Autumn 2001): 321–45.

Anderson, Michael F., ed. *A Gathering of Grand Canyon Historians: Ideas, Arguments, and First-Person Accounts.* Grand Canyon, Ariz.: Grand Canyon Association, 2005.

———. "Grand Canyon National Park Toll Roads and Trails." In *A Gathering of Grand Canyon Historians: Ideas, Arguments, and First-Person Accounts.* Edited by Michael F. Anderson. Grand Canyon, Ariz.: Grand Canyon Association, 2005.

———. *Living at the Edge: Explorers, Exploiters, and Settlers of the Grand Canyon Region.* Grand Canyon, Ariz.: Grand Canyon Association, 1998.

———. *Polishing the Jewel: An Administrative History of Grand Canyon National Park.* Grand Canyon, Ariz.: Grand Canyon Association, 2000.

Andrews, Jack, and Susan Amway. "Lost City of the Dead in the Grand Canyon." www.marsearthconnection.com/egyptgc.html. (Accessed May 3, 2005.)

August, Jack L., Jr. "Hydropolitics in the Far Southwest: Carl Hayden, Arizona, and the Fight for the Central Arizona Project." In *A Gathering of Grand Canyon Historians: Ideas, Arguments, and First-Person Accounts.* Edited by Michael F. Anderson. Grand Canyon, Ariz.: Grand Canyon Association, 2005.

Babbitt, Bruce, ed. *Grand Canyon: An Anthology.* Flagstaff, Ariz.: Northland Press, 1978.

"Bad Time for a Hunt: Horning Search amid Very Busy Canyon Weekend." *Arizona Daily Sun* (Flagstaff), July 4, 1992.

Banks, Leo W., and Craig Childs. *Grand Canyon Stories: Then and Now.* Phoenix: Arizona Highways Books, 1999.

Barber, Susan. "Egyptian Artifacts in the Grand Canyon." www.spiritofmaat.com/archive/nov2/gcegypt.htm. (Accessed April 2, 2006.)

Barnes, Christine. *El Tovar at Grand Canyon National Park.* Bend, Ore.: W. W. West, 2001.

Bass, William Wallace. *Adventures in the Canyons of the Colorado.* Grand Canyon, Ariz.: privately printed, 1920.

Berger, Todd R., Tanya H. Lee, and Kerri Quinn. *Insiders' Guide to Grand Canyon and Northern Arizona,* 2nd ed. Guilford, Conn.: Globe Pequot Press, 2004.

Berke, Arnold. *Mary Colter: Architect of the Southwest.* New York: Princeton Architectural Press, 2002.

Blair, William M. "U.S. Drops Plans to Build 2 Dams in Grand Canyon." *New York Times,* February 2, 1967.

"Both Planes Found; No Survivors." *Arizona Daily Sun* (Flagstaff), July 1, 1956.

Briand, Xavier. "Horning: 'Not Guilty.'" *Arizona Daily Sun* (Flagstaff), July 6, 1992.

"Bright Angel Hotel: New Hotel to Be Ready by the First of the Year; Will Be Known as 'El Tovar.'" *Coconino Sun* (Flagstaff), October 1, 1904.

Brodie, Bernard, ed. *The Absolute Weapon: Atomic Power and World Order.* Freeport, N.Y.: Books for Libraries Press, 1972.

Brownridge, Dennis, and Steve Hinchman. "The Grand Canyon Is Just Another Turbine." In *Water in the West: A High Country News Reader.* Edited by Char Miller. Corvallis, Ore.: Oregon State University Press, 2000.

Brune, Bonnie. "Historic River Running." *In A Gathering of Grand Canyon Historians: Ideas, Arguments, and First-Person Accounts.* Edited by Michael F. Anderson. Grand Canyon, Ariz.: Grand Canyon Association, 2005.

"Bureau Error Forces Dam Releases." *Arizona Daily Sun* (Flagstaff), June 24, 1983.

Buris, Roy. "Notes on the 1944 Plane Crash in the Grand Canyon." *The Ol' Pioneer: The Newsletter of the Grand Canyon Pioneers Society,* September 1992.

"C.A.A. Scans Logs for Clues to Crash." *New York Times,* July 2, 1956.

"C.A.B. Names Panel for Inquiry Into Grand Canyon Plane Crash." *New York Times,* July 28, 1956.

"Canyon Climbers Save 3 Army Fliers." *New York Times,* July 1, 1944.

Carmony, Neil, ed. "The Grand Canyon Deer Drive of 1924: The Accounts of Will C. Barnes and Mark E. Musgrave." *Journal of Arizona History* 43, no. 1 (Spring 2002): 41–64.

"Case of the Homicidal Husband." www.fbi.gov/page2/aug05/leb083105.htm. (Accessed April 9, 2006.)

Castagne, Maurice. *Grand Canyon Orphan Mine: Grand Canyon National Park.* Mina, Nev.: privately printed, 2004.

Chappell, Gordon. "Railroad at the Rim: The Origin and Growth of Grand Canyon Village." *Journal of Arizona History* 17, no. 1 (Spring 1976): 89–107.

Childress, David Hatcher. "Archeological Coverups?" www.keelynet .com/unclass/canyon.txt. (Accessed May 3, 2005.)

"City Goes All Out to Aid Rescue." *Arizona Daily Sun* (Flagstaff), July 3, 1956.

Civil Aeronautics Board. "Accident Investigation Report: Trans World Airlines, Inc., Lockheed 1049A, N6902C, and United Air Lines, Inc., Douglas DC-7, N6324C, Grand Canyon, Arizona, June 30, 1956." SA-320, File 1-00900. Released April 17, 1957.

Cline, Pat. "History's Worst Air Disaster." *Arizona Daily Sun* (Flagstaff), July 2, 1956.

———. "Outmoded Flight Control." *Arizona Daily Sun* (Flagstaff), July 20, 1956.

———. "Should Leave Bodies in Canyon." *Arizona Daily Sun* (Flagstaff), July 6, 1956.

CNN.com. "Investigators Say Ailing Killer Confesses with Months to Live." http://archives.cnn.com/2000/US/10/19/deathbed .confession.ap/. (Accessed April 9, 2006.)

"Colorado Release: 92,000 CFS." *Arizona Daily Sun* (Flagstaff), June 28, 1983.

"Colorado River Closed to Tourist Boat Travel." *New York Times,* June 29, 1983.

"Communities Brace for Flooding." *Arizona Daily Sun* (Flagstaff), June 23, 1983.

"Completion of Grand Canyon Railway." *Coconino Sun* (Flagstaff), October 12, 1901.

"Condor Hatchling Sighted." *Williams-Grand Canyon News,* July 13, 2005.

Coppens, Philip. "Canyonitis: Seeing Evidence of Ancient Egypt in the Grand Canyon." www.philipcoppens.com/egyptian canyon.html. (Accessed April 2, 2006.)

Corle, Edwin. *The Story of the Grand Canyon,* 2nd ed. New York: Duell, Sloan and Pierce, 1951.

Coues, Elliott. *On the Trail of a Spanish Pioneer: The Diary and Itinerary of Francisco Garcés in His Travels through Sonora, Arizona, and California.* New York: Francis P. Harper, 1900.

"Counties Get More Flood Money." *Arizona Daily Sun* (Flagstaff), June 27, 1983.

"Counties Prepare for Flood." *Arizona Daily Sun* (Flagstaff), June 16, 1983.

"Couple Say They Saw Two Planes Collide, Stick at Canyon." *Arizona Republic* (Phoenix), August 2, 1956.

"Crashed Planes Off Course" *Arizona Republic* (Phoenix), July 3, 1956.

"Criminal Becomes Folk Hero: Locals Don't Fear Horning." *Arizona Daily Sun* (Flagstaff), June 24, 1992.

Cushing, Frank H. *The Nation of the Willows.* Flagstaff, Ariz.: Northland Press, 1965.

"Daring Voyagers Heard from Again." *Coconino Sun* (Flagstaff), November 17, 1911.

Dawson, Thomas F. *The Grand Canyon: An Article Giving the Credit of First Traversing the Grand Canyon of the Colorado to James White, a Colorado Gold Prospector, Who It Is Claimed Made the Voyage Two Years Previous to the Expedition under the Direction of Maj. J. W. Powell in 1869.* Washington, D.C.: Government Printing Office, 1917. Reprint, Prescott, Ariz.: Five Quail Books, 2001.

Deaver, Bill. "Memorial Services Held for UAL Dead." *Arizona Daily Sun* (Flagstaff), August 2, 1956.

————. "*Sun* Reporter-Photographer Gives Crash Scene Report." *Arizona Daily Sun* (Flagstaff), July 1, 1956.

Dellenbaugh, Frederick S. *A Canyon Voyage: The Narrative of the Second Powell Expedition.* 1908. Reprint, Tucson: University of Arizona Press, 1984.

Dimock, Brad. "Hard Hulls, Hard Knocks, Hard Heads: The Evolution of Hard-Hulled Rowboats in the Grand Canyon." In *A Gathering of Grand Canyon Historians: Ideas, Arguments, and First-Person Accounts.* Edited by Michael F. Anderson. Grand Canyon, Ariz.: Grand Canyon Association, 2005.

————. *Sunk without a Sound: The Tragic Colorado River Honeymoon of Glen and Bessie Hyde.* Flagstaff, Ariz.: Fretwater Press, 2001.

"Divers to Examine Glen Canyon Dam for Damage to Spillway." *Arizona Daily Sun* (Flagstaff), July 6, 1983.

Dobyns, Henry F., and Robert C. Euler. *The Havasupai People.* Phoenix: Indian Tribal Series, 1971.

Dolnick, Edward. *Down the Great Unknown: John Wesley Powell's 1869 Journey of Discovery and Tragedy through the Grand Canyon.* New York: Harper Collins, 2001.

"D. R. Horning: Hero or Heel?" *Arizona Daily Sun* (Flagstaff), June 25, 1992.

Evans, Edna. *Tales from the Grand Canyon: Some True, Some Tall.* Flagstaff, Ariz.: Northland Press, 1985.

"Explorer Kolb Comes Home with Honors." *Coconino Sun* (Flagstaff), April 10, 1914.

Farabee, Charles R. "Butch," Jr. *Death, Daring, and Disaster: Search and Rescue in the National Parks,* rev. ed. Lanham, Md.: Taylor, 2005.

Faught, Andrew. "Horning Left Calling Card." *Arizona Daily Sun* (Flagstaff), June 26, 1992.

Faught, Andrew, and Robert Gehl. "Gone Again: Horning Steals Car, Takes Off." *Arizona Daily Sun* (Flagstaff), June 30, 1992.

"First Bodies Reach Flagstaff." *Arizona Daily Sun* (Flagstaff), July 2, 1956.

Flint, Richard, and Shirley Cushing Flint, eds. *The Coronado Expedition to Tierra Nueva: The 1540–1542 Route across the Southwest.* Niwot, Colo.: University Press of Colorado, 1997.

"Flooding Leaves Path of Destruction." *Arizona Daily Sun* (Flagstaff), June 30, 1983.

"Floodwaters Will Continue for Months." *Arizona Daily Sun* (Flagstaff), July 4, 1983.

Fontana, Bernard L. *Entrada: The Legacy of Spain and Mexico in the United States.* Tucson, Ariz.: Southwest Parks and Monuments Association, 1994.

Fradkin, Philip L. *A River No More: The Colorado River and the West.* New York: Alfred A. Knopf, 1981.

"Freak Weather May Be Cause of Air Crash." *Arizona Daily Sun* (Flagstaff), July 1, 1956.

Gaylord, A. "Into the Grand Canyon and Out Again, by Airplane." In *The Grand Canyon: Early Impressions.* Edited by Paul Schullery. Boulder: Colorado Associated University Press, 1981.

Ghiglieri, Michael P. *First Through Grand Canyon: The Secret Journals and Letters of the 1869 Crew Who Explored the Green and Colorado Rivers.* Flagstaff, Ariz.: Puma Press, 2003.

————. "George Young Bradley: Chronicler of the 1869 John Wesley Powell Expedition down the Green and Colorado Rivers." In *A Gathering of Grand Canyon Historians: Ideas, Arguments, and First-Person Accounts.* Edited by Michael F. Anderson. Grand Canyon, Ariz.: Grand Canyon Association, 2005.

Ghiglieri, Michael P., and Thomas M. Myers. *Over the Edge: Death in Grand Canyon.* Flagstaff, Ariz.: Puma Press, 2001.

"Glen Canyon Dam Water Releases to Increase." *Arizona Daily Sun* (Flagstaff), July 2, 1983.

"The Grand Canyon of the Colorado." *New York Times,* July 7, 1869.

Grattan, Virginia L. *Mary Colter: Builder upon the Red Earth.* Grand Canyon, Ariz.: Grand Canyon Natural History Association, 1992.

"Greater Volume of Water to Be Released." *Arizona Daily Sun* (Flagstaff), June 29, 1983.

"Group Says It Will Trap Burros to Save Them in Grand Canyon." *New York Times,* June 22, 1980.

"Group Starts Safe Removal of Wild Burros at Grand Canyon." *Arizona Daily Sun* (Flagstaff), July 30, 1980.

"Guard Called to Thwart Looters." *Arizona Daily Sun* (Flagstaff), June 27, 1983.

Haitch, Richard. "Wild Burro Airlift." *New York Times,* May 24, 1981.

Hall, Sharlot M. *Sharlot Hall on the Arizona Strip.* Prescott, Ariz.: Sharlot Hall Museum Press, 1999.

Harding, William Barclay. "To Promote Safety in the Skies." *New York Times Magazine,* July 15, 1956.

"Hearing on Canyon Crash Underway." *Arizona Daily Sun* (Flagstaff), August 1, 1956.

"The Helicopter Heroes." *New York Times,* July 11, 1956.

Henry, Marguerite. *Brighty of the Grand Canyon.* Chicago: Rand McNally, 1953.

"Here and Gone: Horning Search Cut Back—Again." *Arizona Daily Sun* (Flagstaff), June 23, 1992.

Hersey, John. *Hiroshima.* New York: Alfred A. Knopf, 1946.

"He's Back: Escapee Seen." *Arizona Daily Sun* (Flagstaff), June 22, 1992.

"High Water Causing Some Problems for Tourist Business on the Colorado." *New York Times,.* June 24, 1983.

"High Water Claims Life." *Arizona Daily Sun* (Flagstaff), June 26, 1983.

Hill, Gladwin. "Air Control Flaw Charged in Crash." *New York Times,* July 6, 1956.

———. "Climbers Seeking Plane Wreckage." *New York Times,* July 5, 1956.

———. "Paint Mark Hints Crash in Mid-Air." *New York Times,* July 4, 1956.

———. "Removal of Air Victims Starts; Wreckage in Canyon Is Studied." *New York Times,* July 3, 1956.

Hirst, Stephen. *I Am the Grand Canyon: The Story of the Havasupai People,* 3rd ed. Grand Canyon, Ariz.: Grand Canyon Association, 2006.

History and Exploration of the Grand Canyon Region. Natural History Bulletin No. 2. Grand Canyon, Ariz.: Grand Canyon Natural History Association, 1935.

"Horning Forced Locals to Aid Him." *Arizona Daily Sun* (Flagstaff), June 30, 1992.

Hudson, Edward. "Aviation: Busy Skies; Disaster in Grand Canyon Points up Problem of Our Crowded Airways." *New York Times,* July 8, 1956.

Hughes, J. Donald. *In the House of Stone and Light: Introduction to the Human History of Grand Canyon.* Grand Canyon, Ariz.: Grand Canyon Natural History Association, 1978.

Ingram, Jeff. *Hijacking a River: A Political History of the Colorado River in the Grand Canyon.* Flagstaff, Ariz.: Vishnu Temple Press, 2003.

"Inquiry on Air Traffic Control Ordered by House Committee." *New York Times,* July 4, 1956.

Ives, Joseph C. *Report Upon the Colorado River of the West.* Washington, D.C.: Government Printing Office, 1861.

Ivins, Molly. "Wild Burros Plucked out of Grand Canyon." *New York Times,* July 30, 1980.

Johns, Leonard G., Gerard F. Downes, and Camille D. Bibles. "Resurrecting Cold Case Serial Homicide Investigations." In *F.B.I. Law Enforcement Bulletin* 74, no. 8 (August 2005). www.fbi.gov/ publications/leb/2005/august2005/august05leb.htm. (Accessed March 3, 2006.)

Johnson, Dirk. "Fugitive Kidnaps 2 and Eludes Search." *New York Times,* July 5, 1992.

———. "Prison Escapee Is Caught after Two-Month Manhunt." *New York Times,* July 6, 1992.

Karpinski, Henry. "Building the Kaibab Trail." www.geocities.com/ shioshya/kaibab.html. (Accessed April 20, 2005.)

Kazy, Ted. "Copter Reaches TWA Crash; Plans Made to Move Bodies." *Arizona Republic* (Phoenix), July 2, 1956.

Keller, Robert H., and Michael F. Turek. *American Indians and National Parks.* Tucson: University of Arizona Press, 1998.

Kolb, Ellsworth. *Through the Grand Canyon from Wyoming to Mexico.* 1914. Reprint, Tucson: University of Arizona Press, 1989.

Kolb, Ellsworth, and Emery Kolb. "Experiences in the Grand Canyon." *National Geographic* XXVI, no. 2 (August 1914): 99–184.

Lavender, David. *River Runners of the Grand Canyon.* Grand Canyon, Ariz.: Grand Canyon Natural History Association, 1985.

Leavengood, Betty. *Grand Canyon Women,* 2nd ed. Grand Canyon, Ariz.: Grand Canyon Association, 2004.

Leshy, John D. *The Mining Law: A Study in Perpetual Motion.* Washington, D.C.: Resources for the Future, 1987.

Lister, Robert H., and Florence C. Lister. *Those Who Came Before,* 2nd ed. Tucson, Ariz.: Southwest Parks and Monuments Association, 1994.

Lynch, Dudley. "Little Has Changed: 15 Years Ago Wednesday the Hudgin Brothers Found What No One Wanted to See." *Arizona* (June 27, 1971): 19–24.

Manners, Robert A., Henry F. Dobyns, and Robert C. Euler. *Havasupai Indians.* New York: Garland, 1974.

"Mass Burial Monday for Plane Dead." *Arizona Republic* (Phoenix), July 5, 1956.

"Mass Burial Site Selected." *Arizona Republic* (Phoenix), July 6, 1956.

Maxa, Christine. "Triumphs of the Condors." *Arizona Highways* 80, no. 6 (June 2004): 30–32.

McPhee, John. *Encounters with the Archdruid.* New York: Farrar, Straus and Giroux, 1971.

Miller, Char. *Water in the West.* Corvallis, Ore.: Oregon State University Press, 2000.

"Mountaineers Salvage United Airliner Wreck." *Arizona Republic* (Phoenix), July 7, 1956.

"Moving Pictures of the Grand Canyon." *Coconino Sun* (Flagstaff), July 5, 1912.

Nielson, John. *Condor: To the Brink and Back—The Life and Times of One Giant Bird.* New York: Harper Collins, 2005.

"No Compassion for Danny Ray." *Arizona Daily Sun* (Flagstaff), July 2, 1992.

"No Large Pieces of Craft Sighted; Charred Rock on Knoll with Bits of Metal and Paint only Remains of DC-7." *New York Times,* July 2, 1956.

"Officer Says Collision Caused Crash." *Arizona Daily Sun* (Flagstaff), July 3, 1956.

"Officials Confident Canyon Flow Will Ease." *Arizona Daily Sun* (Flagstaff), June 29, 1983.

"Officials Stepping Up Plans to Increase Dam Releases." *Arizona Daily Sun* (Flagstaff), June 17, 1983.

Osborn, Sophie A. H. *Condors in Canyon Country: The Return of the California Condor to the Grand Canyon Region.* Grand Canyon, Ariz.: Grand Canyon Association, 2007.

Pace, Michael Dean. "Emery Kolb: Grand Canyon Photographer and Explorer." M.A. thesis, Northern Arizona University, 1982.

"Parachuters Reach Safety of North Rim." *Coconino Sun* (Flagstaff), July 7, 1944.

Parker, O. K. "To the Colorado River in a Metz 22 Speedster." www.geocities.com/shioshya/mertz.html. (Accessed April 20, 2005.)

Pearson, Byron E. *Still the Wild River Runs: Congress, the Sierra Club, and the Fight to Save Grand Canyon.* Tucson: University of Arizona Press, 2002.

People, Land and Water. "Condor Chick Takes Flight." February 2004.

Pierson, Elizabeth. "Former Deejay Suspected of Killing Wives." *Durango* (Colo.) *Herald.* October 5, 2000.

———. "Dying Man Says He Killed Four." *Durango (Colo.) Herald.* October 6, 2000.

"Plane Crash Detective: William Kossuth Andrews." *New York Times,* July 2, 1956.

Powell, John Wesley. *The Exploration of the Colorado River and Its Canyons.* 1875. Reprint, New York: Penguin, 1997.

Purvis, Louis. "Civilian Conservation Corps Company 818: Building the Colorado River Trail." In *A Gathering of Grand Canyon Historians: Ideas, Arguments, and First-Person Accounts.* Edited by Michael F. Anderson. Grand Canyon, Ariz.: Grand Canyon Association, 2005.

———. *The Ace in the Hole: A Brief History of Company 818 of the Civilian Conservation Corps.* Columbus, Ga.: Brentwood Christian Press, 1989.

"Rain Forces More Colorado Releases." *Arizona Daily Sun* (Flagstaff), June 28, 1983.

"Reclamation Bureau Flooding Decisions to Be Investigated." *Arizona Daily Sun* (Flagstaff), July 8, 1983.

Reilly, P. T. "How Deadly Is Big Red." *Utah Historical Quarterly* 37, no. 2 (1969): 254–56.

"Relatives, Friends of UAL Dead Arrive for Grand Canyon Services." *Arizona Daily Sun* (Flagstaff), August 1, 1956.

"Releases to Start." *Arizona Daily Sun* (Flagstaff), June 22, 1983.

"Rescuers Contact Three Fliers Marooned on Isolated Promontory in Grand Canyon and Entire Party Now on Way to Rim." *Arizona Daily Sun* (Flagstaff), June 30, 1944.

Richmond, Al. *Cowboys, Miners, Presidents and Kings: The Story of the Grand Canyon Railway*, 4th ed. Williams, Ariz.: Grand Canyon Railway, 1999.

———. *Rails to the Rim: Milepost Guide to the Grand Canyon Railway*, 4th ed. Williams, Arizona: Grand Canyon Railway, 1998.

———. "Grand Canyon's Railroad Culture." In *A Gathering of Grand Canyon Historians: Ideas, Arguments, and First-Person Accounts*. Edited by Michael F. Anderson. Grand Canyon, Ariz.: Grand Canyon Association, 2005.

———. "Rails at Both Rims." In *A Gathering of Grand Canyon Historians: Ideas, Arguments, and First-Person Accounts*. Edited by Michael F. Anderson. Grand Canyon, Ariz.: Grand Canyon Association, 2005.

Roderick, Lee. "Water, Water Everywhere." *Arizona Daily Sun* (Flagstaff), June 7, 1983.

Rothman, Hal K. *Devil's Bargains: Tourism in the Twentieth-Century American West*. Lawrence, Kan.: University Press of Kansas, 1998.

Rothschild, Becca. "Horning Plans to Defend Himself." *Arizona Daily Sun* (Flagstaff), July 6, 1992.

Russo, John P. *The Kaibab North Deer Herd: Its History, Problems and Management*. Wildlife Bulletin No. 7. Phoenix: State of Arizona Game and Fish Department, 1964.

Sadler, Christa. *Life in Stone: Fossils of the Colorado Plateau.* Grand Canyon, Ariz.: Grand Canyon Association, 2005.

Schill, Karen. "Fear of Horning: Residents Take Precautions." *Arizona Daily Sun* (Flagstaff), July 2, 1992.

———. "Horning Flees Canyon." *Arizona Daily Sun* (Flagstaff), July 5, 1992.

———. "Horning in Canyon." *Arizona Daily Sun* (Flagstaff), June 28, 1992.

———. "Horning Search in High Gear." *Arizona Daily Sun* (Flagstaff), June 29, 1992.

———. "Hunt Still On: Horning Ditches Car; Eludes Law." *Arizona Daily Sun* (Flagstaff), July 1, 1992.

———. "Sheriff: Convict in Park." *Arizona Daily Sun* (Flagstaff), July 3, 1992.

———. "Tourists Get Surprise." *Arizona Daily Sun* (Flagstaff), June 28, 1992.

Schroeder, John. "Searchers Find Woman Lost 20 Days in Canyon." *Arizona Republic* (Phoenix), August 21, 1975.

Schubert, Frank N. *Vanguard of Expansion: Army Engineers in the Trans-Mississippi West, 1819–1879.* Washington, D.C.: U.S. Department of the Army, Office of the Chief of Engineers, Office of Administrative Services, Historical Division, 1980.

Schwartz, Virginia. "Memorial Service for United Dead Planned Thursday; Rites Will Be Held at Grand Canyon Site." *Arizona Daily Sun* (Flagstaff), July 27, 1956.

"Sheriff Searches for Three Men of Bomber Crew." *Coconino Sun* (Flagstaff), June 23, 1944.

Shuster, Alvin. "Air Traffic Problem Dramatized by Crash." *New York Times,* July 8, 1956.

————. "Visual Rules Put Pilot on His Own." *New York Times,* July 3, 1956.

"Sight-Seeing Called Cause of 2 Crashes." *New York Times,* July 19, 1956.

"Sight-Seeing Hinted as Air Crash Cause." *New York Times,* July 16, 1956.

"Signals from Canyon Spur Fliers' Rescuers." *Arizona Republic* (Phoenix), June 28, 1944.

Silvius, Ray, and Ted Kazy. "Airliner Collision Feared; Wreckage Found in Canyon." *Arizona Republic* (Phoenix), July 1, 1956.

"Sketches of Victims in the Air Crash." *New York Times,* July 2, 1956.

Smith, Dwight L., ed. *The Photographer and the River, 1889–1890: The Colorado Cañon Diary of Franklin A. Nims with the Brown-Stanton Railroad Survey Expedition.* Santa Fe, N.M.: Stagecoach Press, 1967.

Smith, Dwight L., and C. Gregory Compton. *The Colorado River Survey: Robert B. Stanton and the Denver, Colorado & Pacific Railroad.* Salt Lake City: Howe Brothers, 1987.

"Sobs Punctuate Relatives' Vigil for Lost Planes." *Arizona Republic* (Phoenix), July 2, 1956.

Stanton, Robert Brewster. *Colorado River Controversies.* 1932. Reprint, Boulder City, Nev.: Westwater Books, 1982.

————. *Down the Colorado.* Norman, Okla.: University of Oklahoma Press, 1965.

————. "Through the Grand Cañon of the Colorado." *Scribner's Magazine* 8 (November 1890): 591–613.

"State Braces for Flooding." *Arizona Daily Sun* (Flagstaff), June 26, 1983.

Stegner, Wallace. *Beyond the Hundredth Meridian: John Wesley Powell and the Second Opening of the West.* 1954. Reprint, New York: Penguin, 1992.

Strong, Douglas H. "Ralph H. Cameron and the Grand Canyon." *Arizona and the West* 20, no. 1 (Spring 1978): 41–64, no. 2 (Summer 1978): 155–72.

"*Sun* Employee Among First to See Wreck." *Arizona Daily Sun* (Flagstaff), July 1, 1956.

Suran, William C. *The Kolb Brothers of Grand Canyon.* Grand Canyon, Ariz.: Grand Canyon Natural History Association, 1991.

————, ed. *The Brave Ones: The Journals and Letters of the 1911–1912 Expedition down the Green and Colorado Rivers by Ellsworth L. and Emery C. Kolb.* Flagstaff, Ariz.: Fretwater Press, 2003.

————. "With the Wings of an Angel: A Biography of Ellsworth and Emery Kolb." www.grandcanyonhistory.org/kolb.html. (Accessed October 21, 2005.)

"Suspect Loose." *Arizona Daily Sun* (Flagstaff), June 27, 1992.

Sutphen, Debra. "Grandview, Hermit, and South Kaibab Trails: Linking the Past, Present and Future at the Grand Canyon of the

Colorado, 1890–1990." M.A. thesis, Northern Arizona University, 1991.

Sweitzer, Paul. "Nurse Plans to Return to See Havasupai Falls." *Arizona Daily Sun* (Flagstaff), August 21, 1975.

———. "She Took the Wrong Turn." *Arizona Daily Sun* (Flagstaff), August 21, 1975.

"Swiss Flying to Canyon; Wreckage Shows Airliners Collided." *Arizona Republic* (Phoenix), July 4, 1956.

"Swiss to Send Rescue Squad." *New York Times,* July 4, 1956.

"Swollen River Trims Tourism." *Arizona Daily Sun* (Flagstaff), July 1, 1983.

Taylor, Karen L. *Grand Canyon's Long-Eared Taxi.* Grand Canyon, Ariz.: Grand Canyon Association, 1992.

"Three Stranded Fliers on Way out of Canyon." *Arizona Republic* (Phoenix), June 30, 1944.

Thybony, Scott. *Phantom Ranch.* Grand Canyon, Ariz.: Grand Canyon Association, 2001.

"Tragic Crashes Write End to Happy Vacation Dreams." *Arizona Republic* (Phoenix), July 2, 1956.

"Two Airliners Carrying 128 Vanish in the West; Wreckage of One Sighted in Grand Canyon." *New York Times,* July 1, 1956.

Walker, Bonnie. "River Runners Are in a Bind." *Arizona Daily Sun* (Flagstaff), June 26, 1983.

Warren, Ronald L. "Aviation at Grand Canyon: A 75-Year History." *Journal of Arizona History* 36, no. 2 (Summer 1995): 151–72.

Wayman, Ken. "Four Caskets Holding United Victims' Remains Buried at Canyon Cemetery." *Arizona Daily Sun* (Flagstaff), July 12, 1956.

————. "No Hope of Recovering All Bodies; Swiss Mountaineers to Scale Peak." *Arizona Daily Sun* (Flagstaff), July 3, 1956.

————. "Some TWA Passengers Probably Cremated." *Arizona Daily Sun* (Flagstaff), July 6, 1956.

————. "TWA Crash Victims to Lie in Common Grave in Flag Cemetery; May Abandon Rescue Efforts for UAL Dead." *Arizona Daily Sun* (Flagstaff), July 4, 1956.

————. "United Identifies 29 of the 58 Who Died in Grand Canyon Crash." *Arizona Daily Sun* (Flagstaff), July 10, 1956.

"When Rapids Want You, They Get You." *Arizona Daily Sun* (Flagstaff), June 30, 1983.

"When the Averages Fail." *New York Times,* July 2, 1956.

Wolf, T. J. "How Lake Powell Almost Broke Free of Glen Canyon Dam." In *Water in the West: A High Country News Reader.* Edited by Char Miller. Corvallis, Ore.: Oregon State University Press, 2000.

Womack, Capt. James. "'There Was Body of a Boy About 10.'" *Arizona Republic* (Phoenix), July 3, 1956.

"Woman Tells of Seeing Crash Smoke." *Arizona Daily Sun* (Flagstaff), August 3, 1956.

"World of Water and Power in Canyon." *Coconino Sun* (Flagstaff), November 14, 1913.

Wren, Larry. "Gory Crash Scene Detailed by Larry Wren." *Arizona Daily Sun* (Flagstaff), July 4, 1956.

Young, Christian C. "A History of the Kaibab Deer." http://depts .alverno.edu/nsmt/youngcc/research/kaibab/story1.html. (Accessed March 15, 2005.)

———. *In the Absence of Predators: Conservation and Controversy on the Colorado Plateau.* Lincoln, Neb.: University of Nebraska Press, 2002.

INDEX

ABOUT THE AUTHOR

Todd R. Berger is the managing editor of the Grand Canyon Association, where he edits and writes articles, books, and other publications about the Grand Canyon and the surrounding region. Berger is also the author of the *Insiders' Guide to Grand Canyon and Northern Arizona* (2004), the *Insiders' Guide to the Twin Cities* (2003), and *Lighthouses of the Great Lakes* (2002). In addition, he is the editor of eleven anthologies on subjects ranging from golden retrievers to loons. His writing has been published in *Arizona Highways, Williams-Grand Canyon News, Plateau Journal, Canyon Views,* and *The Ol' Pioneer* (the newsletter of the Grand Canyon Historical Society). He serves on the board of directors of the Grand Canyon Historical Society, the Grand Canyon Community Library, and the Publishers' Association of the West. He served on the 2007 Grand Canyon History Symposium planning committee. Berger and his wife, Bonnie, live in Grand Canyon Village.